Praise for
*Beyond Fundamentalism*

"Aslan's new book—his second, after the bestselling *No god but God*, about the origins and evolution of Islam—provides more than just historical precedent; it also offers a very persuasive argument for the best way to counter jihadism and its many splinter groups, such as al-Qaeda."
—*The Washington Post*

"Insightful . . . well-argued . . . tracks the history of antiestablishment thinking in the Islamic world, and explains that al Qaeda is really a social movement for Muslim middle-class youth."
—*The Daily Beast*

"[*Beyond Fundamentalism*] reaches across a world chasm that too many regard as unbridgeable—with balance, eloquence, and rare wisdom."
—JAMES CARROLL, author of *Constantine's Sword*

"[Aslan's] book asks all the important questions. . . . Writing with a critical sense of urgency, Aslan wants us to bring struggles between religious outlooks down from the skies."
—*Slate*

"Eloquent . . . Up-and-coming populist thinker Reza Aslan wastes no time in his . . . thesis to dismantle what he refers to as myths that some Americans believe about everything from Islamo-fascism to jihad."
—*Roll Call*

"Aslan makes the case that the War on Terror is an unwinnable one, precisely because it is the wrong war to fight. A war between religions, a battle between good and evil, a 'cosmic war,' fails to address the underlying social and political roots of conflict and terror. For people of faith and all those concerned with peace in our world, Aslan's exacting prose and depth of discernment create an enticing and necessary read."
—JIM WALLIS, author of *The Great Awakening*

# BEYOND
# FUNDAMENTALISM

ALSO BY REZA ASLAN

*No god but God*

# BEYOND
# FUNDAMENTALISM

*Confronting Religious Extremism
in the Age of Globalization*

## Reza Aslan

Originally published as *How to Win a Cosmic War*

RANDOM HOUSE TRADE PAPERBACKS

NEW YORK

2010 Random House Trade Paperback Edition

Copyright © 2009, 2010 by Aslan Media, Inc.

Published in the United States by Random House,
an imprint of The Random House Publishing Group,
a division of Random House, Inc., New York.

RANDOM HOUSE TRADE PAPERBACKS and colophon are
trademarks of Random House, Inc.

Originally published in hardcover and in slightly different form as
*How to Win a Cosmic War* in the United States by Random House,
an imprint of The Random House Publishing Group,
a division of Random House, Inc., in 2009.

LIBRARY OF CONGRESS CATALOGING-IN-PUBLICATION DATA
Aslan, Reza.
Beyond fundamentalism : Confronting religious extremism in the age of globalization / Reza Aslan.
p.  cm.
ISBN 978-0-8129-7830-8
eBook ISBN 978-0-679-60424-2
1. Jihad.   2. Islamic fundamentalism.   3. War on Terrorism, 2001–
4. Globalization.   I. Title.
BP182.A6 2009
320.5'57—dc22     2008049246

Printed in the United States of America

www.atrandom.com

2 4 6 8 9 7 5 3 1

*Book design by Dana Leigh Blanchette*

# Contents

*Part Three*
## THE END OF THE WAR
## AS WE KNOW IT

# BEYOND
# FUNDAMENTALISM

# Introduction

## Us Versus Them

After the towers had buckled and collapsed and the concussive shock—the raw, unfiltered reality of it all—had settled along with the rubble and ash, a curious document was discovered in the baggage of one of the 9/11 hijackers, detailing the final instructions for carrying out their gruesome sacrifice. I say sacrifice because the anonymous document reads like the script of a ceremonial rite, every mindful act, every rehearsed moment meant to underscore the ritual drama taking place in the minds of the hijackers.

*Purify your soul from all unclean things*, the hijackers were told. *Tame your soul. Convince it. Make it understand. Completely forget something called "this world."*

*Pray the supplication as you leave your hotel. Pray the supplication when riding in the taxi, when entering the airport. Before you step aboard the plane, pray the supplication. At the moment of death, pray.*

*Bless your body with verses of scripture. Rub the verses on your lug-*

*gage, your clothes, your passport. Polish your knife with the verses, and
be sure the blade is sharp; you must not discomfort your sacrifice.*

*Remember they may be stronger than you, but their equipment,
their security, their technology—nothing will keep you from your task.
How many small groups have defeated big groups by the will of God?*

*Remember, this is a battle for the sake of God. The enemy are the al-
lies of Satan, the brothers of the Devil. Do not fear them, for the believer fears only God.*

*And when the hour approaches, welcome death for the sake of God.
With your last breath remember God. Make your final words "There is
no god but God!"*

There is, in these final instructions, a grotesque yet inescapable
truth. The hijackers who murdered more than three thousand souls on
that September morning were carrying out a liturgical act. They cast
their victims as sacrificial lambs being forcibly led to slaughter. They
framed the event in cosmic terms, as *a battle for the sake of God.* In all
things, they strove to maintain their purity—from the moment they
awoke to the moment of their deaths and the deaths of their victims.
Their faith was their strength.

The events of 9/11 by no means inaugurated the debate over religion and violence in the modern world, but they did render the issue
unavoidable. It is easy to blame religion for acts of violence carried out
in religion's name, easier still to comb through scripture for bits of sav-
agery and assume a simple causality between the text and the deed.
But no religion is inherently violent or peaceful; *people* are violent or
peaceful.

Still, these men were Muslim, and their vicious crime does not
negate that fact. Islam may be neither a religion of peace nor a religion
of war but simply a religion like any other, inspiring both compassion
and depravity, but these men read the Qur'an and assured themselves
that it was not innocents they were sacrificing but *the allies of Satan, the
brothers of the Devil.* Whatever else may have been at stake, whatever
social or political motivations may have been behind their abominable

act, there can be no doubt that these nineteen men believed they were acting in the service of God. They were engaged in a metaphysical conflict, not between armies or nations but between the angels of light and the demons of darkness. They were fighting a *cosmic war*, not against the American imperium but against the eternal forces of evil.

A cosmic war is a religious war. It is a conflict in which God is believed to be directly engaged on one side over the other. Unlike a holy war—an earthly battle between rival religious groups—a cosmic war is like a ritual drama in which participants act out on earth a battle they believe is actually taking place in the heavens. It is, in other words, both a real, physical struggle in this world and an imagined, moral encounter in the world beyond. The conflict may be real and the carnage material, but the war itself is being waged on a spiritual plane; we humans are merely actors in a divine script written by God.

A cosmic war transforms those who should be considered butchers and thugs into soldiers sanctioned by God. It turns victims into sacrifices and justifies the most depraved acts of destruction because it does not abide by human conceptions of morality. What use does the cosmic warrior have for such ethical concerns when he is simply a puppet in the hands of God?

A cosmic war is won not through artifice or strategy but rather through the power of faith. Cosmic warriors need not be burdened with tactical concerns such as force of arms or strength of men. It is enough to align one's will with the will of God, to strike at the enemy with the full force of God's wrath, confident that the end rests not in the hands of men.

A cosmic war partitions the world into black and white, good and evil, us and them. In such a war, there is no middle ground; everyone must choose a side. Soldier and civilian, combatant and noncombatant, aggressor and bystander—all the traditional divisions that serve as markers in a real war break down in cosmic wars. It is a simple equation: if you are not *us*, you must be *them*. If you are *them*, you are the enemy and must be destroyed.

Such uncompromising bifurcation not only dehumanizes the enemy, it demonizes the enemy, so that the battle is waged not against opposing nations or their soldiers or even their citizens but against Satan and his evil minions. After all, if we are on the side of good, they must be on the side of evil. And so the ultimate goal of a cosmic war is not to defeat an earthly force but to vanquish evil itself, which ensures that a cosmic war remains an absolute, eternal, unending, and ultimately unwinnable conflict.

Of course, if a cosmic war is unwinnable, it is also unlosable. Cosmic wars are fought not over land or politics but over identity. At stake is one's very sense of self in an indeterminate world. In such a war, losing means the loss of faith, and that is unthinkable. There can be no compromise in a cosmic war. There can be no negotiation, no settlement, no surrender.

The men who attacked the United States on September 11, 2001, were fighting a cosmic war. Any hesitation they might have had about carrying out such an immoral and un-Islamic act was quieted by their firm conviction that it was not they but God who was directing their actions. These were not men lashing out at an occupying power that had left them jobless and hopeless. They were not dispossessed, marginalized, or poor. They attacked the United States not to advance a particular cause or to redress a specific wrong but, as religion scholar Bruce Lincoln notes, simply to make a point, to demonstrate that, "all appearances to the contrary notwithstanding, [they] possessed a power infinitely superior to their adversary's and of an entirely different order."

*How many small groups have defeated big groups by the will of God?*

To be sure, those responsible for the attacks of 9/11 have unveiled a litany of grievances against the United States and the Western world: the suffering of the Palestinians, U.S. support for Arab dictators, the presence of foreign troops in Muslim lands. These may be legitimate grievances. But for the Jihadists, they are more symbolic than real. They are not policies to be addressed or problems to be solved but abstract ideas to rally around. At no point did the hijackers assume their assault on the World Trade Center and the Pentagon would bring peace to Palestine or result in the removal of U.S. troops from the Middle East; in fact, they hoped it would bring *more* troops to the region.

These cosmic warriors, it must be understood, are fighting a war of the imagination. They are waging a battle they know cannot be won in any real or measurable terms. That is not to say that they have no goals. On the contrary, their goal is nothing less than global transformation. But how such a transformation will take shape, who will lead the new order, and what that order will ultimately look like are questions that need not be addressed until after this world has been swept away. That is why they so rarely speak of achieving any kind of "victory," at least not in the sense of enacting some specific social or political agenda. Despite the anxious cries of alarm about an impending global takeover by radical religious groups such as al-Qaʻida, it is remarkable how infrequently these groups make such claims themselves. In all of bin Laden's writings, speeches, and declarations, for example, no attempt is ever made to provide anything akin to an alternative social program. There are no proposals, no policies, no plans, nothing save for a hazy commitment, embedded in al-Qaʻida's constitution, to "establish the truth, and get rid of evil." Indeed, the zealous devotion to the glories of martyrdom that so indelibly marks an organization like al-Qaʻida is itself an implicit recognition that its objectives, unformed and indeterminate as they may be, are impossible to achieve in this life. Al-Qaʻida knows it is incapable of erasing all borders and reestablishing a worldwide Caliphate.* It will never seize control over the Arab and Muslim world. It cannot defeat the United States, let alone dispel its influence from the region. It has no hope of "wiping Israel off the map."

That these absurd ambitions have been embedded in our public consciousness, despite their sheer lunacy, has far less to do with the capabilities of al-Qaʻida terrorists than with the awe-inspiring efficacy of

---

*The political office of the titular head of Islam, established with the death of the Prophet Muhammad in 632 C.E. and abolished by Mustafa Kemal Atatürk in 1924.

the terrorism industry, a term coined by the political scientist John Mueller to describe the nexus of political, military, economic, media, and religious interests that, for a variety of disparate reasons, seeks to convince Americans that "terrorists can strike at any place, at any time, and with virtually any weapon," to quote the Department of Homeland Security manifesto.

Ignoring for a moment that a person is more likely to be struck by lightning than killed by a terrorist, what such breathless declarations reveal is how effective terrorism can be in providing the illusion of power, in giving the impression that the terrorists' goals, no matter how preposterous, are nevertheless achievable. They are not, of course. And in that fundamental truth lies the purpose and power of cosmic war: it provides hope for victory when none exists. All the cosmic warrior need do is *forget something called "this world"* and focus his sights on the world beyond.

If those responsible for 9/11 can be said to have had a single overriding ambition, it was, in bin Laden's words, to "unite the Muslim world in the face of the Christian Crusade" and to maintain, at any cost, the perpetuation of their cosmic war, for there is no more definite means through which their identity can be sustained. As the sociologist Mark Juergensmeyer, who coined the term "cosmic war," writes, "to live in a state of war is to live in a world in which individuals know who they are, why they have suffered, by whose hand they have been humiliated, and at what expense they have persevered."

The attacks of 9/11 have been called a declaration of war. The truth is, they were an invitation to a war already in progress—a cosmic war that, in the religious imagination, has been raging between the forces of good and evil since the beginning of time. It was an invitation that America's own cosmic warriors were more than willing to accept.

Eric Hoffer, writing just after the horrors of a world war against one fanatical ideology—Nazism—and just before the start of a cold war against another—Stalinism—wrote, "In normal times a democratic nation is an institutionalized association of more or less free individuals. When its existence is threatened and it has to unify its people and generate in them a spirit of utmost self-sacrifice, the democratic nation must transform itself into something akin to a militant church or a revolutionary party."

Almost within moments of the attacks on the World Trade Center and Pentagon, that transformation had begun in America.

*These are not normal times.* The popular Christian minister and co-writer of the *Left Behind* series, Tim LaHaye, whose influence over evangelicals is immeasurable, gave voice to millions of Americans when he declared September 11 to be "the focal point of end-time events."

*This is not a normal war.* Our very identity as a nation was at stake. The world had been cleft in two, with good on one side and evil on the other, and victory would come, George W. Bush promised, only when we "rid the world of evil."

*This is not a normal enemy.* "This is a transcendent evil that wants to destroy everything we stand for and believe in," declared Senator John McCain. It is an enemy that, we were told, "think[s] the opposite of the way we think." Lieutenant General William G. Boykin, former deputy undersecretary of defense for intelligence and the man who had been charged with hunting down bin Laden, was more specific. "Our enemy is a spiritual enemy because we are a nation of believers," he told an evangelical congregation in Oregon. "His name is Satan. . . . Satan wants to destroy us as a nation and he wants to destroy us as a Christian Army."

They are the opposite of us. This is a metaphysical conflict. Ethical restraints must be set aside (read: *torture*). The enemy is neither an army nor a state but evil itself. The battle is over civilization. Our identity is at risk. We cannot negotiate. We cannot surrender. We cannot lose.

Nor can we win. In fact, by adopting the religiously charged rhetoric and cosmic worldview of groups like al-Qaʿida, by viewing such terrorist organizations as a demonic force bent on destroying human civilization instead of as an international criminal conspiracy to be brought to justice—in short, by treating the Global War on Terror like a cosmic war—we have not only played into the hands of these radical Muslim militants, we may have set the groundwork for a new and terrifying age of religious war.

That is because despite all the confident predictions one hears about the death of God, the truth is that religion is a stronger, more global force today than it has been in generations. At the dawn of the twentieth century, one half of the world's population identified itself as Catholic, Protestant, Muslim, or Hindu. One hundred years of social progress, technological innovation, and scientific advancement, and that number now stands at nearly two thirds. And while the number of self-professed atheists is also on the rise throughout the world (as is the number of people who profess belief in God yet do not affiliate with any particular religious tradition), of those who do belong to a specific church or religious sect, it is the convervative and fundamentalist believers who outnumber, and increasingly outpace, the moderates and liberals.

How to explain this surge in religious identities? It may have partly to do with the failure of secular nationalism—the core ideological principle of the nineteenth and twentieth centuries—to live up to its promises of global peace and prosperity. Though it is true that religion has been responsible for unspeakable crimes throughout history, it is equally true that the most bestial acts of violence in the last hundred years have been carried out in the name of unabashedly secularist ideologies: fascism, Nazism, Maoism, Stalinism, socialism, even Darwinism. If secularism arose in the eighteenth and nineteenth centuries in response to the erosion of religious certainties, perhaps the rise of religious identities can be blamed on the growing disillusionment with secularism.

Yet there is more to it than this. Globalization has radically altered the way people define themselves, both individually and as a collective.

Across the globe, secular nationalism is beginning to give way to new forms of nationalism based on ethnicity, tribe, and above all religion. In an increasingly globalized world, where the old demarcations of nation-states are slowly starting to give way, religion can no longer be viewed as simply a set of myths and rituals to be experienced in private. Religion is *identity*. Indeed, in many parts of the world religion is fast becoming the supreme identity, encompassing and even superseding ethnicity, culture, and nationality.

In a world where religion and politics are increasingly sharing the same vocabulary and functioning in the same sphere, one could argue that religious grievances are no less valid than political grievances and religious violence no less rational than political violence. This means that cosmic wars can sometimes be political wars, in that they may be not only about the obligation to the next world but also about transforming this one. With this one caveat: political wars can come to an end, political grievances can be settled; cosmic wars are eternal wars, without winner or loser.

To truly confront the radical and fundamentalist forces that, with the precipitous rise of globalization and the steady decline of secular nationalism, have permeated the Jewish, Christian, and Muslim traditions, and which now threaten to plunge the globe into a century of cosmic war, we must strip the conflicts of our world of their religious connotations; we must reject the religiously polarizing rhetoric of our leaders and of our enemies; we must focus on the material matters at stake; and we must seek to address the earthly issues that always lie behind the cosmic impulse. For although the grievances of the hijackers may have been symbolic, though they may have been merely causes to rally around, to the hundreds of millions of Muslims around the world who watched the towers fall—who were, in fact, the intended audience of that theatrical display of violence—they are nonetheless legitimate grievances and must be addressed as such. The Palestinians really are suffering under Israeli occupation. Arab dictators are in fact being propped up by U.S. policies. The Muslim world truly does have reason

to feel under attack by a "crusading" West. Addressing these grievances may not satisfy the cosmic warriors of our world, be they Muslim, Jewish, or Christian. But it will bring their cosmic war back down
to earth, where it can be confronted more constructively. Because in
the end, there is only one way to win a cosmic war: refuse to fight in it.

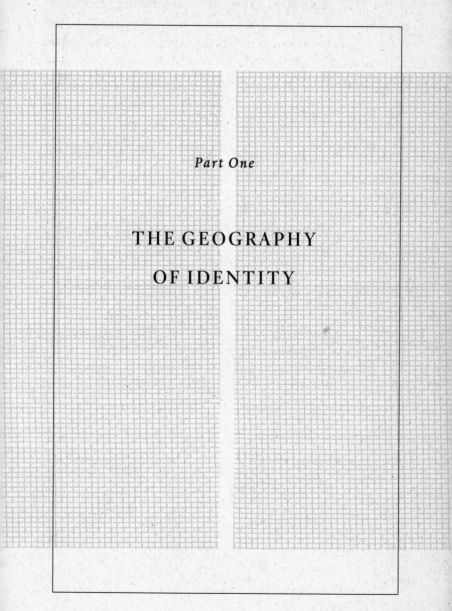

*Part One*

# THE GEOGRAPHY
# OF IDENTITY

CHAPTER ONE

# The Borderless Self

Ben-Gurion International Airport is a brash, beautiful, strikingly confident construction that, like much of Tel Aviv, looks as though it might have sprouted fully formed from the desert sands of the old Arab port city of Jaffa. Named after the surly general and chief architect of the state, the airport is a testament to Israel's self-ascribed position as a bastion of social and technological advancement amid a sea of inchoate enemies. In fact, Ben-Gurion's primary function seems to be to filter out those very enemies by tightly controlling access to the state. This is true of all international airports, I suppose, as anyone who has undergone the humiliation of being scanned, fingerprinted, and photographed to be allowed entry into the United States post-9/11 can attest. In the modern world, airports have become a kind of identity directory: the place where we are most determinately defined, registered, and catalogued before being apportioned into separate queues, each according to nationality.

Still, Israel has, for obvious reasons, taken this process to new and unprecedented heights. I am not two steps off the plane when I am immediately tagged and separated from the rush of passengers by a pimpled immigration officer in a knitted yarmulke.

"Passport, please," he barks. "Why are you here?"

I cannot tell him the truth: I want to sneak into Gaza, which has been sealed off for months. In 2006, when Palestinians were offered their first taste of a free and fair election, they voted overwhelmingly for the religious nationalists of Hamas over the more secular yet seemingly inept politicians of Fatah, the party founded by Yasir Arafat in 1958. Despite having promised to allow the Palestinians self-determination, Israel, the United States, and the European powers quickly decided that Hamas, whose founding charter refuses to recognize the state of Israel and whose militant wing, the Izz ad-Din al-Qassam Brigades, has been responsible for countless Israeli military and civilian deaths, would not be allowed to govern. Gaza, the sliver of fallow land that has become Hamas's de facto stronghold, was cut off from the outside world. International aid dried up and a plan was put in place to, as *The New York Times* put it, "starve the Palestinian Authority of money and international connections" to the point where new elections would have to be held. This resulted in a violent rift between Hamas and Fatah that split the Occupied Territories in two: the West Bank, governed by Fatah with the aid of Israel and the international community, and Gaza, ruled by Hamas and isolated from the rest of the world, a prison with one and a half million hungry, fuming inmates.

I wanted to visit the ruined village of Um al-Nasr, in northern Gaza, some miles away from lush Tel Aviv. A few months earlier, a number of villagers, including two toddlers, had drowned in what the press was calling a "sewage tsunami." The deluge had been triggered by the collapse of a treatment facility just above the village that had been slowly and steadily leaking sewage. For months the villagers of Um al-Nasr had pleaded with Israeli authorities to allow the importation of the pumps, pipes, and filters necessary to stem the flow. But Israel, rattled by a ceaseless barrage of crudely constructed rockets launched daily from Gaza, some of which were—in the sort of grim irony that can exist only in such a place—constructed from old sewage pipes, refused.

The villagers built an earthen embankment around what was fast becoming a giant lake of human waste. But the embankment would not hold. On the morning of March 27, 2007, while most of the villagers of Um al-Nasr slept, the embankment gave way. The village was inundated.

This is what we talk about when we talk about Gaza: that human beings—men, women, children—could literally drown in shit.

"Why are you here?"

"To visit the sites," I say.

It is not a satisfactory answer, and I am taken into a windowless room, where the question is repeated, this time by a slightly older officer. An hour passes, and a third officer walks in with the same question. "Why are you here?"

Thereafter, the question is repeated—in the sterile immigration office; in a smaller, even more sterile office inside the first office; in an even smaller office inside that office; and later, at the immigration queue, at the baggage claim, at customs—until I come to think of "Why are you here?" as a form of greeting.

All of this is understandable. I resent none of it. Though I am a citizen of the United States, I was born in Iran and have spent a great deal of time in countries that do not even recognize Israel's right to exist—countries that, were I to have an Israeli stamp on my passport, would not allow me to enter their borders, would maybe even cart me off to jail. Israel has every reason to be cautious, considering the battering it has received at the hands of people who look just like me.

The problem is not with Israel. The problem is with me, with the sum of my identities. My citizenship is American; my nationality, Iranian; my ethnicity, Persian; my culture, Middle Eastern; my religion, Muslim; my gender, male. All the multiple signifiers of my identity—*the things that make me who I am*—are in one way or another viewed as a threat to the endless procession of perfectly pleasant, perfectly reasonable immigration officers whose task it is to maintain a safe distance between people like them and people like me.

Even so, throughout the entire exercise, I could not help but think of the famed French theorist Ernest Renan, who years ago defined the nation as "a group of people united in a mistaken view about the past and a hatred of their neighbors." Nowhere is that sentiment borne out more fully or with more force than among the relatively new nations scattered along the broad horizon of the Middle East. Perhaps it should come as no surprise, then, that the region in which nationalism arose so late, and so often through the will of others, is the region in which it is now being most unmistakably subsumed by the rising tide of globalization.

Globalization means many things to many people. Though the term itself is new, having entered our vocabulary only in the 1980s, the systemic social, economic, and cultural changes that the word conjures have been taking place for centuries. There is a compelling case to be made for considering the process of globalization to have begun when the first humans footslogged out of Africa in search of game and refuge and more temperate climates. The age of empires was in some ways the height of globalization; the Romans, Byzantines, Persians, and Mongols were able to cross-pollinate their trade, communication, and cultures across vast distances with fluidity and ease. The same could be said of the age of colonialism, in which the old imperial model of commercial relations among neighboring kingdoms was transformed into the more manageable, if less ethical, model of total economic domination of indigenous populations. And certainly no single force can be said to have had a greater impact on propelling globalization forward than religion, which has always sought to spread its message across the boundaries of borders, clans, and ethnicities. Simply put, globalization is not a new phenomenon.

In its contemporary usage, however, the term "globalization" refers to modern trends such as the expansion of international financial systems, the interconnectedness of national interests, the rise of global media and communication technologies like the Internet, and the mass migration of peoples—all taking place across the boundaries of sovereign nation-states. The simplest and most elegant definition of modern globalization belongs to the Danish political philosophers Hans-Henrik Holm and Georg Sørensen: "The intensification of economic, political, social and cultural relations across borders." But I prefer the sociologist Roland Robertson's view of globalization as "a concept that refers both to the compression of the world and the *intensification of consciousness of the world as a whole*" (italics mine).

Globalization is not just about technological advancement and transnational relations. It is about one's sense of self in a world that is increasingly being viewed as a single space. The world has not changed as much as we have. Our idea of the self has expanded. How we identify ourselves as part of a social collective, how we conceive of our public spaces, how we interact with like-minded individuals, how we determine our religious and political leaders, how we think even about categories of religion and politics—everything about how we define ourselves both as individuals and as members of a larger society is transformed in a globalized world because our sense of self is not constrained by territorial boundaries. And since the self is composed of multiple markers of identity—nationality, class, gender, religion, ethnicity, and so on—if one of those starts to give way (say, nationality), it is only natural that another (religion, ethnicity) would come to fill the vacuum.

For most of the last century, secular nationalism—the political philosophy that places the nation-state at the center of collective identity—has been the dominant marker of identity in much of the world, even in the developing world, whose leaders tend to view the creation of a sturdy national identity as the first step in a country's economic and political advancement. Nationalism begins, of course, with the idea of the nation, but the nation is not always so easy to define.

A nation is "a community of common descent," writes Anthony Smith, the foremost theorist on the subject, bound together by a set of shared values and traditions, myths and historical memories, and often linked to some ancestral homeland: "the place where 'our' sages, saints, and heroes lived, worked, prayed, and fought." A state is the bureaucratic mechanism (i.e., government) necessary to organize and control a nation within territorial boundaries. A state has borders; it can be geographically defined. A nation is borderless; it is an "imagined community," to borrow a much-borrowed phrase from Benedict Anderson. The only borders a nation has are those of inclusion and exclusion: who belongs and who does not.

In a state, membership is defined through citizenship. But membership in a nation requires some other measure of unity: the members must share the same traditions, speak the same language, worship the same god, or practice the same rituals. The modern state can be traced back only to the eighteenth century. But the nation has existed from the moment human populations began to organize themselves as families, clans, tribes, *peoples*. The Celts, the Aztecs, the Persians, the Jews, the Arabs—all laid claim to a degree of "nationhood," all possessed a sense of community, and all maintained links to an ancestral homeland long before they were absorbed into various states.

Think of the nation as a grand historical narrative—both mythical and real—written in the memories of generation after generation of a people. The state is the cover and binding that harnesses that narrative, creating a readable book. Thus, when we speak of the nation-state, we refer to the relatively new idea that a nation—a community of common descent—can be contained within the territorial or bureaucratic boundaries of a state. And when we speak of secular nationalism, we mean the even newer idea that the members of a nation-state should be bound together not by religious or ethnic affiliation but through a social contract among free and equal citizens.

When the nation-state was an autonomous, territorially bounded entity governing a community of people who shared some measure of cultural homogeneity—as was the case throughout much of the nineteenth and twentieth centuries—secular nationalism thrived. But globalization has changed everything. The rise of cosmopolitan cities such as New York, Paris, Amsterdam, London, and Hong Kong; the surge in mass migration, dual nationalities, and hyphenated identities; the ceaseless flow of peoples across state borders; all of these have made achieving anything like cultural homogeneity within territorial boundaries almost impossible. The more the world becomes deterritorial-ized, the more nationalism loses its place as the primary marker of col-lective identity. Just as a narrative cannot be truly contained within the bindings of a book, so has globalization put the lie to the idea that a na-tion can be truly bound by the geography of a state.

The truth is that secular nationalism was a shaky idea from the start, one born in post-Reformation Europe, cultivated during the European Enlightenment, then systematically imposed upon the rest of the globe through conquest and colonialism. In large parts of the develop-ing world, the nation-state is a foreign concept. The map of the Middle East is a palimpsest, with arbitrary borders, made-up names, and fabri-cated nationalities often aggressively imposed by colonizers. In this re-gion, nationalism has never been the primary marker of collective identity. Most Sudanese do not refer to themselves as "Sudanese." Rwandan identity is based chiefly on the clan, not the state. Whatever their citizenship, a great many Sikhs will always view their national home to be Khalistan. The Kurds have never been a territorially bounded population, and Iraq is a fictive state built upon the myths and memories of peoples with whom modern-day Iraqis have little in common. In these countries, among these "nations," citizenship is just a piece of paper. And, as Edmund Burke noted a century ago, "men are not tied to one another by papers and seals [but] by resemblances, by conformities, by sympathies."

Even in Europe and the developed world, the idea of secular nation-alism was problematic. That is because membership, or rather citizen-ship, in the nation-state requires submission to the state's sovereignty over all aspects of life. Max Weber's famed axiom that the state is the entity that claims a monopoly on the legitimate use of force has proven a woefully inadequate description of the nearly absolute powers claimed by even the freest and most liberal nation-state. The modern state holds a monopoly not only on force but also on identity. It as-sumes meticulous control over every level of social life, both private and public. It is the primary repressive force for controlling human impulses. It declares what is and what is not proper religious or political expression. It demands consent over all activity—social, sexual, and spiritual. Above all, it decides who can and who cannot share in the collective identity it has itself demarcated. The state's sovereignty over life and death is absolute and unavoidable.

As one can imagine, not all members of a nation have been willing to allow the state to draw boundaries around them, call them a people, a religion, a culture, and thus enforce upon them a categorical sameness to the exclusion of others who may share many aspects of their identity but who happen not to be bounded by the same geography. In all parts of the world, loyalties to family, clan, ethnicity, and religion tend to trump loyalty to the state. Now that globalization has, at the very least, begun to loosen the grip of secular nationalism on our identities, people are beginning to reassemble around older, more primal forms of identity such as religion and ethnicity, neither of which can be easily controlled by the state apparatus.

Witness the fragmentation of the former Yugoslavia. The forced disaggregation of a people once united by a civic identity into tiny, ethnically homogeneous states, each in conflict with the others, is perhaps the clearest example of what happens when transnational identities—in this case ethnicity—clash with national loyalties. Similar tensions led to the partitioning of Urdu-speaking West Pakistan and Bengali-speaking East Pakistan into the homogenized states of Pakistan and Bangladesh. But when it comes to the power of transnational identities to challenge nationalist ones, no force exerts a greater pull than religion.

Fatah learned this truth the hard way. The party of Yasir Arafat began its political career as merely the most formidable of a number of Palestinian underground guerrilla groups active in Egypt and Jordan, but it quickly rose to dominate the Palestinian Liberation Organization, or PLO, the sole legitimate body representing the interests of the Palestinian nation. Fatah's initial success was a result of its ability to unite all the disparate and often feuding Palestinian political groups under a single, secular national identity.

However, the same force that propelled Fatah to the top of Palestinian politics in the 1960s and 1970s—secular nationalism—is the force that has led to its slow demise (though it must be said that the unbridled corruption of many Fatah leaders certainly played a part). In 1988, when, after two decades of crushing occupation the Palestinian population suddenly rose up in open revolt, a new organization, the Islamic Resistance Movement—popularly known by its Arabic acronym, Hamas—burst onto the political scene. In direct opposition to the secular nationalism offered by Fatah, Hamas framed its political platform in exclusively religious terms. It relied on the widely recognized symbols and terminology of Islam to create a new collective identity, one that could cut across all boundaries of culture and class and unite the Palestinian people in resistance to Israel.

In the Muslim world, the fusing of religion and nationalism is called "Islamism." Developed primarily in postcolonial Egypt and India, Islamism is a political philosophy that seeks to establish an Islamic state—either through grassroots social and political activism or through violent revolution—built upon a distinctly Islamic moral framework. Some Islamist groups, such as the Muslim Brotherhood in Egypt, the Islamic Action Front in Jordan, Turkey's Justice and Development Party (AKP), and Algeria's Front Islamique du Salut (FIS), are committed to civic, even democratic, participation in society. Others, such as the Taliban in Afghanistan, Islamic Jihad in Egypt, and the Algerian Armed Islamic Group (GIA), wish to overturn their governments through armed revolt.

Religious nationalism is by no means a uniquely Islamic phenomenon. As we shall see the civil war between Fatah and Hamas (between secular and religious nationalism) is a battle that is taking place all over the globe and in nearly every major religion. This is due partly to the fact that secular nationalism, in demanding that the nation-state be placed at the center of collective identity, was consciously conceived of as an *alternative* to religion. A great deal of nationalism's success in the first half of the twentieth century came from its ability to co-opt the vocabulary, authority, and resources of religious institutions for its own ends. It was perhaps inevitable that, as secular nationalism began to give way, religion would once again become the principal marker of collective identity—and with a vengeance.

The problem with religious nationalism is not its aspirations, which in most cases involve little more than injecting (or perhaps imposing) a particular set of values and customs into society. The problem is that religious identities cannot be tethered to the nation-state. That is why the greatest threat to global security comes not so much from the rise of religious nationalism, which, at least in a democracy, may be unavoidable and which, given space and time, may evolve into mature and responsible governance, as has been the case with Turkey's AKP or, for that matter, many of Europe's Christian Nationalist parties—the real threat to global peace and security comes from the rise of religious *transnationalist* movements that cannot be contained within any territorial boundaries. And the most dangerous by far of these new transnational movements is the broad-based, global ideology of militant Islamic puritanism, of which al-Qa'ida is merely the most notorious and violent manifestation: Jihadism (Global Jihadism, to be precise).

There has been much confusion over the meaning and application of the word "Jihadism" (*jahadiyyah* in Arabic), especially because it is so often misappropriated either by opportunistic politicians who place all of America's adversaries into a single category or by careless media that too often pander to the fears of an unknowledgeable public. Muslims in particular are annoyed by the term, arguing (correctly) that the concept of jihad, as utilized by al-Qa'ida and like-minded militants, is a base and corrupt rendering of a centuries-old doctrine that, in any case, was never one of Islam's principal tenets. In Arabic, *jihad* literally means "struggle" (from the verb *jahada*, meaning "to strive for something") and is almost always followed in the Qur'an by the phrase "in the way of God." Jihad implies a struggle against the self, against one's passions and instincts and the temptations that oppress the soul. Yet in a religion obsessed with social justice, the idea of jihad as an internal struggle quickly expanded to include the physical struggle against oppression, against chaos and civil strife, against the internal and external enemies of Islam, even against unbelief.

For the Jihadist, however, the doctrine of jihad transcends these traditional definitions, becoming instead a means of devotion. The Jihadist movement, in bin Laden's words, "wants to keep jihad alive and active and make it part of the daily life of Muslims. *It wants to give it the status of worship.*" For Maulana Masood Azhar, the head of the Kashmiri Jihadist organization Jaish-e Muhammad, jihad is not only "the most virtuous deed," it is, in fact, "the protector of all other deeds." The pillars of faith and practice upon which Islam is founded—prayer, alms, fasting, pilgrimage, and the confession of faith—are, in Jihadism, supplanted by the one and only means of salvation: jihad. "Everyone not performing jihad today is forsaking a duty," wrote the father of modern Jihadism, Abdullah Azzam, "just like the one who eats during the days of Ramadan without excuse, or the rich person who withholds the *zakah* [alms] from his wealth. Nay, the state of the person who abandons jihad is more severe." It is not scripture, nor theology, nor prayer, nor good works, nor the law, nor any spiritual endeavor that defines a Muslim but, as Azzam declared, "jihad and the rifle alone."

Despite its fixation on jihad, Global Jihadism is less a religious movement than it is a social movement, one that employs religious symbols to forge a collective identity across borders and boundaries (more on this later). Jihadism traces its historical roots not to the Prophet Muhammad but to the Arab anticolonialists of the twentieth century, men like Hasan al-Banna and Sayyid Qutb. It looks not to the Qur'an for its doctrinal basis but to the writings of the thirteenth-century legal scholar Ahmad ibn Taymiyyah. It has more in common with the Bolsheviks and the French revolutionaries than it does with militant Muslim nationalist groups such as Hamas and Hizballah. To talk about Jihadism as Islamofascism is to misunderstand both Jihadism and fascism. Fascism is an ideology of ultranationalism; Jihadism rejects the very concept of the nation-state as anathema to Islam. In that regard, Jihadism is the opposite of Islamism.

It is ironic that Jihadism is so often viewed as antimodern. Jihadism does not reject modernity; it is a product of modernity. It does, however, reject Westernism, and because "modernity" and "the West" have become inextricably linked (mostly in the West), anyone who rejects one is automatically assumed to reject the other. Jihadism may present itself as an alternative to the modern world, but the ideas upon which it draws are quintessentially modern. To paraphrase the British political philosopher John Gray, Jihadism is "a symptom of the disease of which it pretends to be the cure."

Neither is Jihadism traditionalist. Jihadist ideologues go to great lengths to distance themselves from the traditional doctrines of Islam. There is in this movement a complete rejection of Islamic authority and an almost total disregard for Islamic law. In the United States and Europe it is common to point the finger of blame for the radicalization of Muslim youth at mosques and madrassas (Islamic schools). But that assumption ignores the seismic societal shifts that globalization has wrought upon the Arab and Muslim worlds over the last century, as widespread increases in literacy and education, not to mention the birth of new technologies such as satellite TV and the Internet, have allowed Jihadist leaders to sidestep Islam's traditional clerical authorities and deliver their individualistic, anti-institutional message directly to Muslims all over the globe.

Nowhere is Jihadism's lack of regard for Islamic tradition more obvious than in its fundamental reimagining of the doctrine of jihad. What was for centuries considered a collective duty waged predominantly within the confines of an empire or state and solely in defense of life, faith, and property ("Fight in the way of God those who fight you," the Qu'ran warns, "but do not begin hostilities; God does not like the aggressor"; 2:190), has, in Jihadism, become a radically individualistic obligation utterly divorced from any institutional power (the Yemeni Sheikh Rabi al-Madkhali defines a Jihadist as "anyone who believes that Jihad is purely an individual duty to fight"). Indeed, the fundamental aim of Jihadism is to separate the doctrine of jihad from all political or religious institutions, so as to make it strictly an *ethical* obligation. This is not jihad in its classical Qur'anic sense as a struggle against oppression ("permission to fight is given only to those who have been oppressed;" 22:39). This is something else entirely. This is jihad as a form of identity—a mere metaphysical struggle stripped of all political considerations.

This is jihad as cosmic war.

Jarret Brachman, the director of the Combating Terrorism Center at West Point, traces Jihadism's current incarnation as a global force to about 2003, though its roots go back to an early-twentieth-century Islamic revivalist movement known as Salafism (the term *salaf* refers to the original Companions of the Prophet Muhammad). Salafism began as a progressive movement in colonial Egypt and India whose adherents advocated reform and liberalization of traditional Islamic doctrine. The movement was founded upon the writings of two of the century's most renowned Muslim intellectuals, the Iranian scholar/activist Jamal ad-Din al-Afghani (who began his career in India) and the Egyptian reformer Muhammad Abdu. Al-Afghani and Abdu believed that the only way for the Muslim world to throw off the yoke of colonialism and push back against Western cultural hegemony was through a revival of Islam. These "modernists," as they were called, blamed the clerical establishment—the *'ulama*—for the sorry state of Muslim society. They sought to challenge the clergy's self-proclaimed role as the sole legitimate interpreters of Islam by advocating an individualized, unmediated, and highly personal reading of the Qur'an and the Hadith (the collected sayings and actions of the Prophet Muhammad).

By far the most successful Salafist organization of the time was the Muslim Brotherhood. Founded in the 1920s by the Egyptian schoolteacher turned activist Hasan al-Banna, the Muslim Brotherhood began as a grassroots social movement dedicated to the gradual Islamization of society through religious welfare and education programs. Al-Banna believed that the only way to create a truly Islamic state was through preaching and good works, not, as some of his fellow Islamists argued, through violence and armed revolt. Although far more conservative in his interpretation of Islam than either al-Afghani or Muhammad Abdu, al-Banna nevertheless agreed that the main obstacle facing an Islamic revival was the *'ulama,* or, more specifically, the senior clergy of Egypt's famed al-Azhar University, whose international prestige and longevity (it was established a thousand years ago) have made it the closest thing the Muslim world has to a Vatican. In fact, al-Banna explicitly established the Muslim Brotherhood as an alternative source for Muslim spirituality, one whose reformist outlook and social activism created a stark contrast to the somewhat stilted theology offered by the clergy of al-Azhar.

By the time Hasan al-Banna died in 1949, the Muslim Brotherhood was the most dominant social movement in Egypt. Indeed, after the collapse of the Ottoman Caliphate in 1924—the symbol of the global Muslim community, or *ummah*—the Muslim Brotherhood was the only truly transnational Islamic movement in the world, with offshoots in Syria, Jordan, Palestine, and Lebanon. When, in 1952, a group of Egyptian military officers led by Colonel Gamal Abd al-Nasser launched a coup against Egypt's British-backed monarchy, the Muslim Brotherhood helped rally the country under the new regime. At first Nasser welcomed the Brotherhood into his administration, placing its members in a number of senior government posts. But after a failed attempt on his life, allegedly by a member of the Brotherhood, Nasser outlawed the organization altogether and threw its leaders into jail.

In prison, the Brotherhood fractured into competing groups. A new breed of activists, led by the charismatic Egyptian academic Sayyid Qutb, transformed al-Banna's social movement into a revolutionary force dedicated to "setting up the kingdom of God on earth and eliminating the kingdom of man." Qutb argued that Nasser—and in fact every other Arab leader—could not be considered a true Muslim unless he was willing to strictly apply and abide by Islamic law (known as Shariah). And since he was unwilling to do so, he was an apostate, a *kafir;* his punishment was death. Qutb went so far as to state that anyone who accepted Nasser's leadership was also a *kafir.* "Those who consider themselves Muslim, but do not struggle against different kinds of oppression, or defend the rights of the oppressed, or cry out in the face of a dictator, are either wrong, or hypocritical, or ignorant of the precepts of Islam," Qutb declared.

Nasser executed Qutb in 1966, but by then Qutb's influence had spread through the ranks of the Muslim Brotherhood, radicalizing the Salafist movement. Fearing for their lives, the Qutb-inspired Salafists and radical members of the Muslim Brotherhood (Qutbists, they are sometimes called) fled their home countries in Egypt, Syria, Jordan, and Palestine for the only place that would give them refuge, Saudi Arabia. There they encountered an even more conservative strain of Islam commonly called Wahhabism.

Born in the vast desert wastelands of eastern Arabia, a region known as the Najd, Wahhabism (its adherents prefer the term "Muwahiddun," meaning "Unitarians") is a militantly puritanical movement founded by Muhammad ibn Abd al-Wahhab in the middle of the eighteenth century. Claiming that the purity of Islam had been defiled by "un-Is-lamic" beliefs and practices such as praying to saints and visiting their tombs, Abd al-Wahhab sought to strip Islam of what he considered to be its cultural, ethnic, and religious "innovations" (*bida'*), so as to re-store the faith to its original, unadulterated, and distinctly *Arab* origins.

In 1932, just as the discovery of oil began to reshape both the phys-ical and the social landscape of the Arabian Peninsula, Wahhabism be-came the official religion of the Kingdom of Saudi Arabia. By the 1960s, the kingdom had become one of the richest countries in the world. Massive skyscrapers towered over traditional city centers, as in Mecca. The city of Jeddah, in western Saudi Arabia, had transformed itself into an international hub for business and finance. To keep oppo-sition (particularly religious opposition) in check, the Saudi regime co-opted the Wahhabi clergy to give the royals religious sanction for whatever they wished to do. This had the result of pushing young Saudis—many of whom had been born into an internationally isolated and ultraconservative society but who were suddenly finding them-selves trying to cope with an increasingly opulent, cosmopolitan coun-try awash in "Western cash" and swayed by "Western values"—away from the traditional religious authorities and into the hands of the Qutbists and radical Salafists who quickly dominated the intellectual circles of Saudi Arabia. It was the hybridization of Salafism and Wahhabism—of Islamic political activism and Saudi puritanism—that would give birth to a new, ultraconservative, ultraviolent social movement of young Muslims properly termed Jihadism.

At first, Jihadism began as just another Islamist movement focused on establishing an Islamic state. As Fawaz Gerges, America's premier scholar of Jihadism, has shown, the early Jihadists were "religious nationalists whose fundamental goal was to effect revolutionary change in their own society." Their primary focus was on what they termed the "Near Enemy"—Arab regimes, "hypocrite" imams, apostate Muslims—as opposed to the "Far Enemy"—Israel, Europe, and the United States. "The road to Jerusalem goes through Cairo," Ayman Zawahiri wrote in 1995, before he had joined al-Qaʿida, when he was still a fervent Islamist and the head of a religious nationalist organization known as Egyptian Islamic Jihad (EIJ).

Throughout the 1980s and 1990s, however, Zawahiri and a great many of his fellow Jihadists began gradually to shift their focus from the Near Enemy to the Far Enemy—from localism to globalism. This was partly a result of the failure of Islamism to bring about the revolution it had promised for so long. The violent suppression of religious nationalism throughout the Arab world had effectively broken the back of the Islamist movement. In Algeria, parliamentary elections were canceled by the military when it appeared that the Islamists of the Front Islamique du Salut (FIS) might win a majority of the seats. The FIS, which had caused a stir in Islamist circles by participating in democratic elections, was swiftly outlawed and its leaders were imprisoned. The result was a devastating civil war that cost the lives of nearly 200,000 people, convincing Algeria's more radical Islamist groups, such as the Armed Islamic Group, or GIA, that political participation was a waste of time. Around the same time, an offshoot of the Muslim Brotherhood called the Combatant Vanguard launched a rebellion in the Syrian city of Hama. In response, Syria's president, Hafez al-Assad, unleashed the full force of his army upon the town, killing tens of thousands of Muslim Brothers and virtually razing Hama. Abu Musab al-Suri, the al-Qaʿida ideologue who was a member of the Combatant Vanguard but who was not one of the rebels, wrote in his memoirs that the massacre at Hama, more than anything else, made him realize that Islamism was doomed to fail. Meanwhile, the Egyptian branch of the Muslim Brotherhood had abandoned its military activities and, under severe pressure from the government, reformulated itself as a political party ready to engage the establishment rather than to fight it. The Salafist groups that remained uninfluenced by Saudi Wahhabism soon began to follow the lead of the Egyptian Muslim Brotherhood, publicly renouncing violence and returning to their roots of preaching and social welfare (though, unlike the Brotherhood, the Salafists refused to enter the political arena). By the end of the 1990s, scholars such as Olivier Roy and Gilles Kepel were confidently pronouncing the death of Islamism as a viable political ideology.

Yet, beyond the seeming failure of Islamism, there was a far more significant development in the globalization of the Jihadist movement. The Soviet invasion of Afghanistan in 1979 drew to the region a wave of Jihadists from every corner of the world, many of whom, like Zawahiri and al-Suri, felt increasingly abandoned by the collapse of the Islamist movements in their own countries. The presence on the battlefield of tens of thousands of Muslim fighters from Egypt, Saudi Arabia, Syria, Yemen, Palestine, Algeria, Sudan, Tunisia, Iraq, Pakistan, Jordan, Malaysia, Indonesia—all working together for a common cause—created a sense of global community among the Jihadists that they had never before experienced. In his memoirs, Nasir Ahmad al-Bahri, who would eventually become one of bin Laden's chief bodyguards, described a similar feeling of communal identity among the Jihadists fighting in Bosnia: "We realized we were a nation [*ummah*] that had a distinguished place among nations. Otherwise what would make me leave Saudi Arabia—and I am of Yemeni origin—to go and fight in Bosnia? The issue of nationalism was put out of our minds, and we acquired a wider view than that, namely the issue of the *ummah*."

After the war, when the fighters returned to their home countries, they discovered that they were no longer as animated by local concerns as before. To some, the idea of building an Islamic state seemed somehow antiquated. "The struggle to establish the Islamic state cannot just be fought on a regional level," declared a suddenly globally minded Zawahiri in December 2001, after he had merged his nationalist group, Egyptian Islamic Jihad, with Osama bin Laden's al-Qa'ida. In Afghanistan, but also in Bosnia and Chechnya, the Sudan and Somalia, the Jihadists had been given a glimpse of a borderless future where nationality, citizenship, ethnicity, and even language were no longer paramount, where the only identity that mattered was religious identity. Their sights were now set firmly on global transformation. Their guns had turned on the Far Enemy.

By the end of the millennium, Islamism and Jihadism, once cousins, had effectively split into two opposing, rival movements: "religious nationalism" versus "religious transnationalism." Today, Islamism remains a nationalist ideology, whereas most Jihadists would like to erase all borders, to eradicate all nationalities, and to return to an idealized past of religious communalism. An Islamist group such as Hizballah has no global agenda. Its money may come from Iran, but its agenda stops at the borders of Lebanon. The same is true of Egypt's Muslim Brotherhood, which diligently portrays itself as a nationalist movement with exclusively nationalist ideals. Jihadism, however, rejects the very concept of nationalism; it is as much an *antinationalist* movement as a *transnationalist* one.

The Islamists of Hamas draw their ranks from the fathers of the children who drowned in the village of Um al-Nasr: the marginalized and dispossessed of society, men and women for whom there seems no future. For members of such groups, social, political, or economic deprivation is often the chief motivation for action.

Not so with Jihadism, which finds its members among the educated, urbane, middle-class Muslim kids living in, say, East London who read about the deaths of the children of Um al-Nasr on the Internet. These young Muslims tend to be socially integrated and politically active but find traditional expressions of Islam—that is, the Islam of their parents—inadequate for confronting the challenges of the modern world. They are bound together by a master narrative of oppression and injustice, convinced of their role in the cosmic war between good and evil.

Islamist groups can sometimes be fearful of globalization, viewing it as a "Western" assault on their religious identity. Jihadism, on the other hand, is the child of globalization; it relies for its very existence on a world without borders, a world in which no barrier exists between religion and politics, between the sacred and the secular. In its drive to reestablish a global Caliphate, Jihadism seeks a deterritorialized Islam—one unrestrained by the boundaries of ethnicity and culture.

Not all Jihadists are globalists, of course, nor do all Islamists confine themselves solely to nationalist concerns (as we shall see, the attacks of September 11, 2001, have led a great many Jihadist leaders to question the viability of focusing so narrowly on the Far Enemy). But for those who continue to count themselves among the growing ranks of the Global Jihadist movement, the strategy of "dragging the Far Enemy onto the battlefield," of expanding the goals and aspirations of Jihadism beyond local grievances, beyond nationalist concerns, the shift in focus from the Near Enemy to the Far Enemy both "resolves the mental complex in the *ummah* with regard to defining the enemy," to quote the Syrian al-Suri, and frames the Jihadist struggle not as a battle between rival political ideologies but as a cosmic contest between belief and unbelief—or, in Zawahiri's words, "between Islam and the infidels." In such a battle, no one can remain neutral. Every Muslim has a duty to respond to the call of jihad, to rally under the banner of Islam, to come to its defense, and to join in a cosmic war whose epicenter lies here, in Israel, at the nexus of nationalist and transnationalist identities, where secular and religious nationalisms collide, often with bloody consequences, where the very concept of cosmic war was born and where, according to Jewish, Christian, and Muslim tradition, the war will come to a final and fiery end.

# CHAPTER TWO

# A Land Twice Promised

Jerusalem. The City of God. What better setting for a cosmic drama?

It is difficult to get one's bearings in this city. Time is variable here. The past and the present—two autonomous threads—are, in Jerusalem, so tightly entwined that they cannot be parsed. The only constant is space: tangible, eternal space. Take away the kabob stands and the gleaming, glass-walled visitor center and this is still the city carved out by Herod two thousand years ago.

History has not been kind to the man called Herod the Great. Best known for his slaughter of Bethlehem's children in a vain search for the infant Jesus—an implausible event attributed to him solely by the Gospel of Matthew, for which there exists not a single corroborating source in any of the other chronicles or histories of the time—Herod is often depicted as a barbarous and licentious half-Jew (his mother was Arab); a greedy libertine more Roman than Jewish; a rapacious bull of a man who seized power through sheer, unbridled sycophancy.

Yet, despite his reputation, it was Herod who built the markets and theaters, the palaces and ports, the *gymnasia*, amphitheaters, and baths that made the city of Jerusalem one of the cosmopolitan jewels of the ancient world. "Ten measures of beauty hath God bestowed upon the world," the Talmud says; "nine of these fall to the lot of Jerusalem."

Herod's greatest achievement was the restoration and expansion of the Temple of Jerusalem, which he had raised atop Mount Moriah—the highest point in the city—and embellished with wide Roman colonnades made of white Jerusalem stone. This was Jerusalem's second temple. The first temple, built by Israel's King Solomon, was destroyed by the Babylonians in 586 B.C. This second temple, built some seventy years later, would be sacked by Rome in 70 C.E., a mere fifty years after Herod finished renovating it, as punishment for a revolt led by a group of wild-eyed revolutionaries called the Zealots.

Today, all that remains of Herod's Temple is a single wall at the western base of Mount Moriah: the Wailing Wall, it is sometimes called, the Kotel. There is nothing special about the wall itself, save for its colossal size. It remains unadorned, unembellished, even unkempt—tufts of thick green caper bushes creep through the cracks and crevices in the ancient stones. But since the destruction of the Second Temple, this wall is now held to be a symbol of God's divine presence in Jerusalem. The Jews who come here with their prayers, who embrace and kiss the stones, are performing more than a religious rite. They are making a political statement. Just as this wall has stood on this ground for thousands of years as witness to the birth of the Jewish nation, so now does it signal that nation's return and permanent presence in the Holy City. The Jews can no more be uprooted from Jerusalem than this mammoth wall can be disinterred from the earth.

On the day I visited the Temple, a large group of cadets from the Israel Defense Forces (IDF) had gathered at the Wailing Wall for prayers. It was a remarkable sight: fresh-faced adolescents of different races and ethnicities, dressed in matching olive-green uniforms, dancing arm in arm with bearded old men clad in black—everyone swaying back and forth together like flickering flames.

Someone tapped me on the shoulder: a pale Orthodox girl, maybe twenty years old.

"Are you Jewish?" she asked. She was wearing a plain white head-scarf.

"No," I replied. "But I get that a lot."

She wasn't disappointed. If anything, her eyes shone brighter. She was a college student from Minneapolis who had taken a week off of school to volunteer for a foundation dedicated, she said, to furthering the Jewish presence in Jerusalem. As we stood together at the wall, she spoke excitedly about its eternal significance to the Jewish people, handing me booklets and fliers and small souvenir trinkets. She had to make me understand. Every fiber of her being vibrated with the need to make me feel what she felt when she stood at this place.

"Let's go to the top," I suggested. "To the Temple Mount."

She recoiled at the thought. Although Orthodox Jews pray daily for the restoration of the Temple, most Orthodox rabbis are adamant that, until the Messiah returns, it is forbidden for a Jew to set foot on the Temple Mount (the platform atop Mount Moriah upon which the Temple was built), lest one accidentally trespass upon the Holy of Holies. A sign posted at the Temple entrance by Israel's Chief Rabbinate reads: *Entrance to the area of the Temple Mount is forbidden to Jews owing to the sacredness of the place.* Few but the most observant Jews take the warning seriously.

"You go up," she said. "I'll wait for you down here."

She pointed me to a line of camera-toting tourists waiting to climb a steep wooden ramp that led up to the Temple Mount. Heavily armed Israeli soldiers guarded the walkway. I had been in line for only a few minutes when one of them pointed at me.

"You," he barked. "You cannot enter. Not with your backpack."

"Everyone here has a backpack."

"The Muslims will not let you on the Mount with a backpack. There is no choice in the matter."

"But I *am* Muslim."

"There is no choice in the matter."

Although Israeli security forces maintain legal jurisdiction over the whole of the Old City, the Temple Mount itself remains under the control of Jerusalem's Muslim authorities (known as the Waqf). Over the years, this delicate balance has been repeatedly tested, most recently in 2000, when the former Likud party prime minister, Ariel Sharon, while locked in a tough parliamentary contest with the current Likud leader, Benjamin Netanyahu, for control of the party, staged a highly provocative visit to the Temple Mount, accompanied by hundreds of Israeli soldiers and police dressed in riot gear. (Sharon is a deeply loathed figure in Palestine for his role in the 1982 massacre of thousands of Palestinian civilians at the Sabra and Shatila refugee camps in Lebanon.) Standing in front of the Wailing Wall, surrounded by armed guards, Sharon declared, "The Temple Mount is in our hands and will remain in our hands. It is the holiest site in Judaism and it is the right of every Jew to visit the Temple Mount."

Rumors quickly spread throughout the Old City that the Jews were attempting to seize the Temple Mount. A crowd of angry Palestinians rushed to the site and began pelting Jewish worshipers with rocks. The Israeli police responded with tear gas; more than thirty people were injured—both Palestinians and Israelis. The incident ignited what came to be known as the second Palestinian uprising, or intifada.* It also helped Sharon defeat Netanyahu in the parliamentary elections.

Not wanting to be separated from my backpack, I withdrew from the line of tourists and scrambled around the Wailing Wall, past the Jewish and Armenian quarters of the Old City, through the Via Dolorosa in the Christian Quarter, and over to the cramped and overcrowded Muslim Quarter, where gates lead directly up to the Dome of the Rock, the annular, porcelain-walled sanctuary that now sits almost exactly where the Temple of Jerusalem once stood. Built some thirteen centuries ago, the Dome of the Rock is not a mosque. The mosque atop the Temple Mount (which Palestinians refer to as Haram al-Sharif) is called al-Aqsa; it is positioned on the southeast corner of the Mount. The Dome of the Rock was originally intended to be an alternative pilgrimage site to Mecca, a way to draw the Muslim faithful

*The first intifada occurred in 1987.

to Jerusalem. Although it is said to house the rock on which the Prophet Muhammad stood before ascending to heaven during his Night Journey, or *Miraj,* to this day the Dome remains, like the Wailing Wall, as much a political site as a religious one—a symbol of the permanent Muslim presence in the Holy City. Images of its glittering gold cupola can be found in every Palestinian household. A picture of the Dome hangs behind the desk of the Palestinian president and head of Fatah. Its silhouette, flanked by two swords, is emblazoned on the seal of Hamas.

Access to this side of the Temple Mount is strictly controlled by the Waqf, who refuse to allow Christians or Jews to congregate in large groups on the site, so worried are they that this prized slab of real estate will be pried away from them. This is not paranoia. Razing the Dome of the Rock in order to build the Third Temple on its ruins has been a goal of more than a few Jewish and Christian radical groups. In 1969, a Christian from Australia sneaked onto the Temple Mount and set fire to the silver-topped al-Aqsa mosque. In 1982, an Israeli soldier stormed into the same mosque brandishing an army-issued M-16 rifle and began shooting worshipers at random. One particularly tenacious radical, Yoel Lerner, has been convicted three times of trying to blow up the Dome of the Rock; at each of his trials, Lerner has openly called for the overthrow of Israel's secular government and its replacement with a Jewish theocracy.

Perhaps the most ambitious attempt to destroy the Dome of the Rock took place in 1984. A Palestinian guard, making his rounds in the early morning, noticed that the gate to the platform had been pried open. He immediately alerted Israeli security forces, who rushed to the site. The intruders were already gone, having scattered at the first hint of trouble. But what they left behind sent shudders throughout the country. Littered around the Dome were hundreds of pounds of explosives, dozens of army-issued grenades, boxes of dynamite, ropes, ladders, knapsacks.

After a two-month investigation, three men were arrested, all of them from the Lifta Valley, a Mediterranean village near Jerusalem, a place of placid springs and terraced gardens. Dubbed "The Lifta Gang" by the Israeli media, the men confessed to being members of a Jewish underground group, some of whom had banded together to destroy the Dome of the Rock and seize control of the Temple Mount with the ultimate aim of rebuilding the Temple, thus preparing the way for the coming of the Messiah.

Had the plan succeeded, it would likely have led to a bloodbath. Of course, that was the point. The Lifta Gang wanted to launch a final confrontation that would sweep up every Jew, Christian, and Muslim in a cosmic battle. When confronted at their trial with the possibility of the Jewish deaths that would have resulted from their actions, the members were unmoved. Revolutions require sacrifices.

Inching my way through the back alleys of the Muslim Quarter, I arrived at the rickety green gates leading to the Dome of the Rock. Two machine-gun toting kids dressed in military fatigues sat at the entrance, eying me cautiously.

"Stop," one of them said in Arabic.

"I only want to pray," I said.

"Are you Muslim?" asked one. "Show me," said the other, before I could respond. I had no idea what he could mean.

"The *Fatiha*," the other said, suddenly inspired. "Give us the *Fatiha*."

I rattled off, in my best Arabic, the opening words of the Qur'an: *"In the name of God the Merciful, the Benevolent. All praise to God, the Lord of the Worlds. . . ."*

"Okay. Okay." The first guard interrupted, this time in English. "Now you give us five dollars."

"Five dollars for what?"

"For watching your backpack, of course. The Jews will not let you take it up there."

So it goes, for decades, for centuries. If a nation is a historical narrative written in the myths and memories of a united people, and the state that narrative's cover and binding, the cosmic war between Israel and Palestine is what happens when two competing national narra-tives—neither of which can be fully harnessed by the state—vie for the same sacred, eternal space.

The story of the state of Israel usually starts like this:

Paris, 1894. A cleaning lady was making her rounds inside the forti-fied German Embassy in the heart of the French capital when she dis-covered a suspicious piece of paper in the wastebasket of the German military attaché, Major Max von Schwartzkoppen. The paper was a *bordereau*—an official memorandum—handwritten in French and ad-dressed to Schwartzkoppen.

"Having no indication that you wish to see me," the memo read, "I am nevertheless forwarding to you, Sir, several interesting items of in-formation."

What followed was a catalog of secret military documents that would be made available to the German major should he wish to have them, including information on French artillery formations and "a note on the hydraulic brake of the 120mm cannon," a new weapon in the French armament.

The memo was unsigned; it was only a promise to make the secret files available for the major at his convenience. However, at the bottom of the page there followed a brief yet incriminating adieu: "I am off to maneuvers."

The cleaning lady understood at once what she held in her hand. "I am off to maneuvers." That could mean only one thing: someone in the army was offering to provide military secrets to the Germans. This was treason! She immediately handed the memo over to French intel-ligence, which wasted no time in accusing a low-ranking general staff officer, a Jew from Alsace named Alfred Dreyfus, with high treason.

There was no evidence for the charge, save for a dubious expert tes-timony linking Dreyfus's handwriting to that of the memo. But no ev-idence was needed. When the charges against Dreyfus were first made public, the head of French intelligence, hearing that Dreyfus was a Jew, summed up the widespread anti-Semitism of the army, and indeed of much of France. "I should have realized," he said.

There was a trial, but it was a farce. Much of the evidence against Dreyfus was forged, and flagrantly so, by the head of army intelligence, Colonel Hubert Henry. The only other evidence necessary for conviction flowed through Dreyfus's veins. He was not French, after all; he was a Jew.

A French court-martial stacked with loyal monarchists and fervent nationalists convicted Dreyfus in a closed and secret session; he was not allowed to see the evidence against him. Despite his repeated protestations, Dreyfus was sentenced to a life of solitary confinement on Devil's Island, the infamous penal colony just off the coast of French Guiana.

It is no accident that the rise of anti-Semitism in nineteenth-century Europe coincided with the rise of nationalism. Nationalism, you will recall, presupposes a measure of ethnic or cultural homogeneity within a nation-state—something to bind a population together under a single collective identity. But the Jews represented a conspicuously alien culture that, despite centuries of living and thriving in every corner of Europe, had, in the minds of many, yet to sufficiently assimilate into European society (at least not enough to have disappeared altogether). The secret trial and false conviction of Alfred Dreyfus was a human tragedy. But the affair also raised much broader issues of national identity among the French. The right-wing newspaper editor Édouard Drumont captured the sentiment of many French nationalists when he declared that Dreyfus's betrayal was the inexorable destiny of his race. The Jews were a nation within a nation; it was inconceivable to think that their loyalties would be to France.

"Out of France, Jews!" Drumont demanded in his widely read periodical *La Libre Parole*. "France for the French!"

Drumont, a fuming, portly, irascible man with a wiry beard that splayed across his chest, is often regarded as the father of modern anti-

Semitism in Europe. His book *La France juive* (*Jewish France*), which provided a disturbing account of the Jewish presence in France, sold a million copies and went through more than one hundred editions in French before being translated for the rest of Europe. Drumont's bigoted argument about "the problem of the Jew in Europe" was, at the time, an outgrowth of the very idea of nationalism, which, as the historian Eric Hobsbawm writes, "by definition excludes from its purview all who do not belong to its own 'nation,' i.e., the vast majority of the human race."

The arduous task of constructing a collective identity, especially one based on something so nebulous as cultural homogeneity, often requires an adversary, an Other, against which to define oneself. Throughout much of Europe, the Jew served as "the negative pole of the nationalist movements," writes Michel Winock in his history of anti-Semitism in France. According to Winock, the Jew became the "revealer" of European national identity, the out-group that gave shape to the in-group. What did it mean to be French or German or Dutch at a time when those identities were only just beginning to be nationalistically defined? It meant not being a Jew.

Not everyone in France followed Drumont's lead, of course. A slew of officers, politicians, judges, lawyers, and intellectuals—most famously the writer Émile Zola, whose celebrated manifesto "J'accuse!," published on the front page of the Paris daily *L'Aurore,* remains a testament to his intellectual heroism—came out in defense of the innocent Dreyfus. Their relentless drive for the truth ultimately set Dreyfus free, though only after he had served five brutal years on Devil's Island. Still, nationalism requires unity, and unity, wrote Ernest Renan, "is always effected by means of brutality." The Dreyfus affair set European nationalism on a course that would ultimately lead to the rise of Nazism and the slaughter of more than six million Jews.

Half a century before that abominable event, however, a number of leading Jewish intellectuals had already come to the realization that assimilation into European culture was futile. They believed they would never share in the imaginary cultural homogeneity being constructed in the burgeoning nation-states of Europe and thus would never find a home on the continent. Drumont was right, some of them thought. The Jews were a nation within a nation. Only by extricating themselves from Europe and establishing their own nation-state could they be truly free of persecution.

It was a fanciful idea, to be sure. Jewish cultural unity was, for a people living in dozens of different countries, difficult to imagine; how on earth would national unity be devised? And, perhaps more problematically, where on earth? The idea of a Jewish nation-state would likely have remained just that had it not been for one of those spectacular historical coincidences. On the day that Dreyfus was taken away to Devil's Island, as he was dragged onto the streets and publicly stripped of his rank to a wild chorus of "Death to the Jews!" "Death to the Judas!," there was, among that rancorous crowd, a young Viennese journalist and amateur playwright who had traveled to Paris to cover the event. His name was Theodor Herzl.

The germ of the idea that blossomed into the state of Israel was actually planted twelve years prior to the Dreyfus affair, in a pamphlet published in Germany by a Polish physician named Leon Pinsker. Titled "Auto-Emancipation," the pamphlet launched Hovevei Zion (Lovers of Zion), a Jewish settler movement and precursor of the nationalist philosophy that would later be known simply as Zionism.

As Pinsker saw it, the "hoary problem" of the Jews—the fact that they could "neither assimilate nor be readily digested by any nation"—was summed up by two fundamental truths: the Jews were dispersed in various countries throughout the world, and in each of those countries, they constituted a persecuted minority. (Pinsker termed this persecution "Judeophobia," recognizing, correctly, the ethnocentric confusion caused by the word "anti-Semitism," since Arabs are also Semites.) Pinsker's solution to this twofold problem was to develop a distinctly Jewish version of nationalism to compete with the surging nationalisms of Europe. That would be no easy task. Pinsker understood that the world's Jews lacked the essential attributes that foster nationalism: a common language, cultural or ethnic homogeneity, consanguinity, and what Pinsker called "cohesion in space." This last point was instrumental. A national identity could never emerge while the Jews were scattered across the globe. "The Jewish people," Pinsker wrote, "has no fatherland of its own, though many motherlands; no center of focus or gravity, no government of its own, no official representation. They are at home everywhere, but are nowhere at home."

The only solution was for the Jews to leave their home countries and gather as one nation inside a new, territorially bounded "fatherland." But even Pinsker recognized the glitch in his proposition: "What land will grant us permission to settle a nation within its borders?" he asked.

Fourteen years later, Theodor Herzl thought he had the answer. Herzl was a student at the University of Vienna when "Auto-Emancipation" was published. Vienna at the time had no shortage of young, nationalistically minded Jewish intellectuals. A schoolmate of Herzl, Nathan Birnbaum, had founded an organization of Jewish nationalists called Kadima (Forward); its purpose was to promote a sense of national unity among the Jews of Europe. It was Birnbaum who coined the word "Zionism" in 1890, but it would be Herzl's earthshaking manifesto, *Der Judenstaat* (*The Jewish State*), published in 1896, that would give the idea substance.

Unlike Birnbaum, Herzl was a thoroughly assimilated, thoroughly secular Jew, fluent in neither Hebrew nor Yiddish (at the time the most commonly spoken language among European Jews) and with no abiding interest in Jewish culture or religion. But he had been utterly transformed by the Dreyfus affair. Witnessing that murderous horde clamoring for an innocent man's blood had convinced him that there was no future for the Jews in Europe; they would have to build a state of their own. Though much has been made about his willingness in later years to compromise on the location of a future Jewish state, there was never any serious doubt—not for Herzl, nor for Birnbaum, nor for the Zionist Congress they together helped found in order to realize their nationalist aspirations—that it would have to be constructed upon the coastal plains and bare valleys of Palestine. Zion is, after all, the biblical name of Jerusalem. "Palestine is our ever-memorable historic homeland," Herzl wrote in *The Jewish State*.

The problem was that a significant population of indigenous Arabs had already been living in Palestine for centuries. A sizable number of Palestinian Jews also lived side by side with the Arabs, but the overwhelming majority of the population was Arab: Jewish, Muslim, and Christian. Not only was the land already settled and under the suzerainty of the Ottoman caliph, who, as one might imagine, was not receptive to the idea of turning it over to Europe's Jews, but Palestine, and Jerusalem in particular, was as sacred to the Arabs as it was to the Jews. When Vienna's rabbis sent a fact-finding mission to determine the feasibility of Herzl's idea, the mission sent back a cable reading "The Bride is beautiful, but she is married to another man."

For Herzl, the solution was self-evident, if a bit problematic. "We must expropriate gently the private property," he wrote in his diary in June 1895, "[and] spirit the penniless population across the border." As the Israeli historian Benny Morris has argued, given that "the vast majority of Palestine's Arabs at the turn of the century were 'poor,' Herzl can only have meant some form of massive transfer of most of the population."

That is precisely what Herzl meant. The calculus was inescapable. The Zionist ideal could be realized only through the creation of a Jewish state in Palestine, and the only way the population of such a state could have a Jewish majority was to remove its non-Jewish inhabitants. The argument was made more succinctly by the true architect of the Jewish state, David Ben-Gurion. "The Arabs will have to go," Ben-Gurion wrote to his son in 1937. The Zionists, it seems, had learned a constructive lesson from European nationalism: unity is always effected by means of brutality.

The Jewish nationalists of the early twentieth century faced a formidable task. How were they to unite a dispersed people of French, German, Iraqi, Russian, Polish, and Romanian descent—separated from one another by miles and by conventions—under a single national identity? That knotty question ultimately tore Birnbaum and Herzl apart. For Birnbaum, Jewish national identity could be based only on cultural unity, perhaps through the use of a common language such as Yiddish. Herzl, who did not speak Yiddish, maintained a broad, somewhat undefined notion of political unity based on a sense of historical memory and territorial integrity. In other words, gather the people together, put a border around them, and a nation-state will arise.

Yet doesn't being a Jew have at least partly to do with a connection to the faith, practice, and religious institutions of Judaism? Early Zionists such as Achad Ha'am thought so. Ha'am started out as a supporter of Pinsker's Hovevei Zion movement but later developed a more explicitly religious definition of Jewish unity that was severely critical of the secular Zionism propounded by Herzl, a man who once described the Jewish religion as "superstition and fanaticism." Meanwhile, Orthodox Jews, for whom Jerusalem was a place of pilgrimage and the locus of messianic aspirations, shuddered at the idea that religious duty to the city should be translated into political sovereignty over it. As far as they were concerned, the Law of Torah was absolutely clear on this point: only the Messiah could reestablish the state of Israel, and only at the end of time. Then there was the rather large contingent of theocratic Jews, who, in contrast to the Orthodox, supported the creation of a Jewish state, but only if it were constructed as a religious state and based on Jewish law. These so-called Religious Zionists, conspicuously absent from the first meeting of the World Zionist Congress, which met in Basel, Switzerland, in 1897, ultimately formed their own religious parties, which to this day remain opposed to the secular nationalism upon which Israel was founded.

Even after the horrors of the Holocaust gave weight to the Zionist argument that assimilation into Europe was impossible, there were still a great many who would not be convinced that the Jewish nation could be—or for that matter should be—contained within a state. What would gather such an ethnically diverse, culturally heterogeneous, religiously disparate, linguistically dissimilar community together under a single, secular, nationalist umbrella?

For Jewish nationalism to survive in Palestine, it needed the "negative pole" spoken of by Michel Winock—the Other against which to define itself as a culturally cohesive, ethnically homogeneous, and nationally united community. With regard to the Jews already beginning to settle in Palestine, that Other quickly took the form of the land's native inhabitants. What did it mean to be a Jewish nationalist in Palestine in the first half of the twentieth century? It meant not being an Arab.

As in Europe, which had to purge "the nation within" in order to fully enable a national identity based on cultural homogeneity, the Zionists carved out a physical space for themselves inside Palestine, then gradually expelled from that space those who could claim no share of Jewish cultural, religious, ethnic, or linguistic heritage. In this way, they fashioned a national identity for a people who had not imagined any such thing in almost two millennia. "With the evacuation of the Arab community from the valleys we achieve, for the first time in our history, a real Jewish state," Ben-Gurion wrote in his diary. "As with a magic wand, all the difficulties and defects that preoccupied us until now in our settlement enterprise [will vanish]."

A carefully constructed narrative began to form among the Zionist leaders: Yes, there was a large Arab population already living in Palestine. *But they were not Palestinian.* They were not a distinct people, a tribe, a *nation*. They could not be considered a national entity. They were part of the global "Arab nation" and thus held no claim to the land on which they lived. As Israel's "Iron Lady," Golda Meir, explained, "It was not as though there was a Palestinian people in Palestine considering itself a Palestinian people and we came and threw them out and took their country away from them. They did not exist."

Hence the Zionist slogan: "A land without a people for a people without a land."

It is true that a firm national consciousness did not exist among the Arabs of Palestine, any more than it did among Palestine's Jews—at least not before the Zionists arrived in droves. At the time nationalism was a distinctly European and secular phenomenon. Although there were upper-class Arab intellectuals and landed elites who considered themselves "Palestinian"—that is, living in a region called Palestine, distinct from a territory called Syria, inside an empire dominated by Turks—the majority of Palestine's Arab Muslim population had, up to that point in time, considered itself subjects of the Ottoman caliph. (Palestine's Christians, however, had a much more developed sense of themselves as Palestinian nationals, and in fact the most vigorous arguments against Zionism came from Christian Arabs.)

Still, the stirrings of Arab nationalism could be felt in hundreds of secret literary societies that had cropped up all over the Ottoman Empire around the same time as Herzl and Birnbaum were meeting in Vienna. The members of these societies sought to carve out a distinctly Arab (and distinctly secular) identity in opposition to Turkish cultural hegemony by reclaiming Arabic as the official language in majority-Arab regions (language being an effective means of fostering national unity). These Arab nationalists were emboldened by the Young Turk Revolution of 1908, in which a coalition of military students, young army officers, and Turkish nationalists staged a coup against the Ottoman caliph, Abdul Hamid II, and initiated a series of constitutional reforms throughout the empire. The reforms did not amount to much, and, in fact, the revolution itself seemed only to have precipitated the demise of the "Sick Man of Europe," as Europeans had dubbed the Ottoman Empire. But the incident convinced Arabs that emancipation from Ottoman control was possible.

That sentiment was nourished during the First World War, when the British promised full independence for much of the Arab world in return for siding with the Allies against the Ottomans. Independence never materialized, of course; the vanquished Ottoman lands were divvied up among the European powers as spoils of war. When the Second World War erupted, the Europeans again guaranteed the

Arabs independence, this time in exchange for help fighting Adolf Hitler. That promise, too, was broken. But those unmet promises, along with the dissolution of the Ottoman Caliphate in 1923, ignited a wave of national consciousness across the Arab world. And although, in countries such as Egypt and Syria, Arab nationalism remained at that point a somewhat shapeless conviction based chiefly on a sense of common culture and shared language, in Palestine, the presence of half a million newly arrived Jewish immigrants made constructing a national identity a much simpler endeavor.

The unintended consequence of Zionism was that it shifted the consciousness of Palestine's Arabs away from the larger pan-Arab exercises in nationalism taking place elsewhere and toward a more finely honed Palestinian identity. Zionism provided Palestinians with their own distinct national narrative. It allowed for a firmer sense of national cohesion than that which existed in most other parts of the Arab world. It created a collective identity based on resistance to occupation—by the Jews as well as by the British. In short, Zionism became for the Arabs in Palestine that much-needed "negative pole." What did it mean to be Palestinian? It meant not being a Jew.

What happened next has been so exhaustively documented and debated that it has ceased being history and has slipped instead into the shadowy realm of historical myth. In 1917, British troops marched into Jerusalem and found themselves in the midst of a civil war between competing claims of nationalism. At first Britain was amenable to the idea of a Jewish state. The Zionist argument that, in the hands of the Jews, Palestine would be "an outpost of culture against barbarism," to quote Herzl—and incidentally a tool with which to further British colonialism in the region—was irresistible. As Arthur Balfour, the British foreign secretary and the namesake of the Balfour Declaration, which promised British support for the state of Israel, claimed, "The four great powers are committed to Zionism, and Zionism, be it right or wrong, good or bad, is rooted in age-long tradition, in present needs, in future hopes, of far profounder import than the desires and prejudices of the . . . Arabs who now inhabit that ancient land."

When at the end of World War II Britain no longer had the will or the means to maintain control over an increasingly riotous, bitterly divided population, the problem of Palestine was handed over to the newly formed United Nations, which split the country in two. On November 29, 1947, the U.N. General Assembly passed Resolution 181, calling for the creation of two separate and distinct states, each containing its own ethnically and religiously homogeneous "nation."

The Palestinians rejected Resolution 181 outright. The geography of the partition was, according to the Arab Higher Committee representing Palestinian demands, "absurd, impracticable, and unjust." The resolution established a serpentine border. It gave the Jews, who at the time owned 7 percent of the land and made up less than a third of the population, 56 percent of the country, seven eighths of the citrus groves, most of the arable fields, and a majority of the Mediterranean ports. Some 80 percent of the land that would be the future state of Israel was still private property owned by Arabs.

A great many Zionists also rejected the partition plan, according to the Israeli historian Avi Shlaim, "as it fell short of the full-blown Zionist aspiration for a state comprising the whole of Palestine and Jerusalem"—what was being referred to as Eretz Yisrael, or "biblical Israel." Menachem Begin—at the time the head of an underground paramilitary organization called the Irgun, later to become prime minister and Nobel Peace Prize winner—summed up the sentiments of many Jewish nationalists when he proclaimed, "The partition of Palestine is illegal. It will never be recognized. Jerusalem was and will forever be our capital. *Eretz Yisrael* will be restored to the people of Israel. All of it. And for ever."

Cooler heads among the Zionists prevailed. Ben-Gurion, ever the pragmatist, recognized the historic opportunity for international legitimacy and accepted U.N. Resolution 181 as, if nothing else, a good start. A decade earlier, when partition had first been discussed among the Zionist leaders, Ben-Gurion had argued, "I am certain we will be able to settle in all the other parts of the country, whether through agreement and mutual understanding with our Arab neighbors or in another way. Erect a Jewish state at once, even if it's not in the whole land. The rest will come in the course of time. It must come."

With the impasse seemingly irresolvable, Europe ravaged by two wars, the United States cocksure and concentrating on the Soviet Union, and the Arab states bungling toward independence, the Zionists unilaterally declared statehood. On May 14, 1948, the state of Israel was born.

The next day, the Arabs declared war.

Six decades have passed since the war Israelis call the War of Independence and Palestinians lament as al-Nakba, "the Catastrophe." Sixty years, five wars, and countless deaths later, the miraculous state of Israel lives on, having taken on all enemies, both internal and external, and, in crushing them, secured an enduring home for the Jewish nation in the middle of the ever-mutable map of the Middle East. Today, Israel is as prosperous and as secure as it has ever been. Its economy is flourishing. Its military is by far the most powerful in the region. It has the best universities and the most educated population in the Middle East. It is a refuge for Jews around the world. More than that, it is a testament to the strength, resilience, and ingenuity of the Jewish people in the face of near-total annihilation.

The state of Palestine, however, is a fading dream. Of the ten million Palestinians in the world, half live as refugees. Any real hope for a unified state has buckled under the weight of the ongoing civil war between Hamas and Fatah, between competing claims of secular and religious nationalism. Today, Gaza is one of the poorest, most densely packed regions on earth, while nearly half of the West Bank is under Israeli control.

To truly appreciate the way in which the two competing national narratives of Israel and Palestine have played out over the last sixty years, stand not in Old Jerusalem, at the majestic Wailing Wall, but in East Jerusalem, at the separation wall built by Israel as a defensive measure to keep Israelis and Palestinians apart. This grotesque barrier of concrete, barbed wire, electric fencing, sniper towers, checkpoints, and barricades will, when completed, be four times as long and in some areas twice as high as the Berlin Wall. The wall has already devoured 140,000 acres of Palestinian land in Jerusalem alone. Ultimately, it will encircle 40 to 50 percent of the West Bank, making the idea of creating a contiguous Palestinian state almost risible. The wall bisects major urban districts, creates ghettos where there were once thriving Palestinian towns, separates farmers from their crops, divides families from their loved ones, and cuts off Palestinians from schools, hospitals, and places of work.

The Israeli government insists that the barrier is necessary to keep Palestinian terrorists out of Israel and, more urgently, to protect hundreds of thousands of Jewish settlers living in more than fifty settlements dotting the Occupied Territories. No doubt suicide attacks in Jerusalem have declined dramatically since construction of the wall began. Yet the great irony is that today, Israel's most profound existential threat comes not from Arab armies or Palestinian militants but from this very wall, or at least from what it represents, not just to Palestinians but to Muslims, Christians, and Jews around the world for whom a territorial conflict between two nation-states has become a contest over the favor of God—a cosmic war that no wall, no matter how long or how high, can contain.

Two years before Mohammed Siddique Khan, the soft-spoken second-generation Pakistani-Briton from West Yorkshire, led three of his friends on a suicide mission that would end in the murder of more than fifty of his fellow British citizens on July 7, 2005, he stood at this wall, at one of its five hundred or so security checkpoints. In all of the material published about the so-called 7/7 bombers, all of the documents and studies and conferences meant to discover what could have led to the radicalization of those four seemingly benign British youths, Khan's trip to Israel is rarely, if ever, mentioned. But there can be little doubt that it was the decisive moment in his young life—the pivot in his journey from husband and father and, by all accounts, well-

adjusted, well-integrated, well-educated youth worker to radical Jihadist bent on mass murder.

Khan's trip occurred as a last-minute detour on his way back to
Britain, after he had completed the Hajj pilgrimage with his wife and a
couple of close friends. As they crossed into Palestinian territory, Khan
witnessed with his own eyes the unbearable weight of degradation carried by a people in no control of their own lives, in no control even of
their movements.

As the story was told to me by one of his companions, Khan had
passed through the crossing, his British passport a ticket to the front of
the line. There he saw an old Palestinian man, a native of this dry patch
of land, being manhandled by a nervous young soldier—an Israeli
probably no older than the pimply immigration officer who had pulled
me aside as I deplaned in Tel Aviv. A second soldier, sweating and tim-
orous and just as young as the first, held a rifle barrel against the old
man's chest. There had been attacks at this crossing in the past: Israelis
had died; *Jews* had died.

The old man lowered his head. He was used to this. He did not
speak as the soldier rummaged through his belongings. Khan stood by,
also saying nothing. But the old man's shame burned hot in his cheeks.

Mohammed Siddique Khan was not an Arab. He had not traveled
extensively through the Arab world, nor, according to his friends, had
he shown much interest in doing so. He had never expressed excessive
solidarity with the plight of the Palestinians; this was his first visit to
the region. Before this trip, he had not even been considered especially
devout.

But in that fateful moment, his identity was altered. He was
no longer British. He was no longer Pakistani. His sense of self could
not be contained by either nationalist designation. He was simply a
*Muslim:* a member of a fractured, imaginary "nation" locked in an
eternal cosmic war with a Jewish "nation" just as imaginary and just as
fractured.

On the way back to Beeston, the drab, isolated inner heart of southern Leeds where Khan and his fellow 7/7 bombers lived, the mild-mannered youth worker shocked his companions by suddenly proclaiming his new identity and, with it, his murderous intention.

"They kill *us*," he cried out, "so we must kill *them*!"

His companions were confused. What did he mean? they wondered. Who is us? Who are them?

Two years later, Khan cleared up any confusion in a video testimony left behind before he performed his heinous act: "Your democratically elected governments continuously perpetuate atrocities against my people all over the world," he accused the British nation-state—*his* nation-state. "And your support of them makes you directly responsible, just as I am directly responsible for protecting and avenging my Muslim brothers and sisters."

We have all have heard these words, or words like them, before. They are common in so-called suicide videos, the visual testimonies Jihadists often leave behind before embarking on their murderous mission. As a transnational social movement, one of Jihadism's greatest challenges is to link together all the disparate identities of its members—regardless of their race, culture, ethnicity, or nationality—under a single collective identity. The easiest way to do this is through what the sociologist William Gamson calls "injustice framing": identify a situation as unjust; assign blame for the injustice; propose a solution for dealing with the injustice and those responsible for it; and then, most important, connect that injustice to a larger frame of meaning so as to communicate a uniform message that will resonate with as much of the population as possible.

Successful framing has the power to translate vague feelings of anger and resentment into tangible, easy-to-define grievances. It can also connect local and global grievances that may have little or nothing to do with one another under a "master frame" that allows a movement's leaders to encompass the wider interests and diverse aspirations of their members.

These so-called "frame alignment techniques" allow social movements like Jihadism to more easily create in-groups and out-groups.

They help identify and, more important, vilify the enemy. They can even assist movement leaders in marking neutral bystanders as either sympathetic or antagonistic to the movement's cause, all with the aim of compelling people to join the movement and *do something* about their grievances. In short, framing helps members of a social movement make the difficult transition from collective identity to collective action. And by far the easiest form of collective action is violence, especially organized and ritualized violence, which can transform complex, multipronged conflicts for which blame may be difficult to apportion into simple, black-and-white ones for which blame is easy to assign: *them.*

There remains today no more potent symbol of injustice in the Muslim imagination than the suffering of Palestinians under Israeli occupation. Particularly in the Arab world, it is hard to find a primary or secondary school where schoolchildren do not learn about the daily misery of boys and girls their own age who, due to circumstances that may be beyond anyone's control but that nonetheless cry out for culpability, do not share in the most basic rights and privileges that they themselves enjoy. In universities, the plight of the Palestinians is as essential a chapter in the study of Arab history as the Civil War is in American history. In some ways, Palestine has become the sole source of pan-Islamic identity in the Muslim world, the universal symbol that, in the absence of a Caliphate, unites all Muslims, regardless of race, nationality, class, or piety, into a single *ummah*—a single community. On a recent trip to Iran, I was struck by a pair of giant paintings emblazoned across a highway overpass. The first depicted the now-famous image, broadcast to the world by the BBC in 2000, of a Palestinian man, Jamil ad-Durra, crouched behind a concrete block, trying in vain to shield his small son from a torrent of bullets fired by Israeli soldiers standing nearby, the image frozen in the instant before the boy was shot dead in his father's arms. The second depicted an even more famous photo: a masked, black-clad Iraqi prisoner at Abu Ghraib, standing barefoot on a box, his arms outstretched as though he were crucified, wires extending from his fingers like electric tendrils.

Under the first painting it read, YESTERDAY PALESTINE; under the second, TODAY IRAQ.

Yet, as undeniably dreadful as the plight of the Palestinians may be, for the Jihadists, Palestine is a mere abstraction, a symbol whose sole purpose is to draw Muslims to their cause. It is not the Palestinian struggle for statehood that animates most Jihadists. As a global ideology, Jihadism is totally detached from such nationalist concerns. Jihadist fighters do not travel to Palestine to fight alongside the militants of Hamas (they would not be welcome if they did). Jihadist ideologues have not formulated any specific plans to address the Palestinian situation, save pushing Israel into the sea (a silly and, as even the Jihadists themselves admit, hopeless notion). It is true that Jihadist leaders such as bin Laden and Zawahiri frequently rail against Israel and the United States for allowing the Palestinians to suffer under Israeli occupation. But such complaints, though legitimate, must be read as part of a much broader catalog of Jihadist grievances, some of which are so random, so mind-bogglingly unfocused, that they should be recognized less as grievances per se than as popular causes to rally around. There are, for instance, protests about the United States' unwillingness to sign on to the International Criminal Court and anger at America's role in global warming. ("You have destroyed nature with your industrial waste and gases," Osama bin Laden writes, "more than any other country. Despite this, you refuse to sign the Kyoto agreement so that you can secure the profit of your greedy companies and industries.") There is bin Laden's inexplicable tirade against America's campaign finance laws, which, as he argues, "favor the rich and wealthy, who hold sway in their political parties, and fund their election campaigns with their gifts." The Jihadists have even launched protests against the widely acknowledged election fraud that took place during the Florida recount in the 2000 presidential election between George W. Bush and Al Gore.

These are not *real* grievances for the Jihadists. (It does not bear mentioning that bin Laden is probably not concerned with campaign finance reform in the United States.) These are, rather, a means of weaving local and global resentments into as wide a net as possible, one that can be spread across borders and boundaries—over all the walls, actual or metaphorical, that divide the *ummah* into states, nationalities, ethnicities, cultures, classes, even genders—to form a single master narrative, a single collective identity; to convince Muslims that their grievances, whatever they may be, are no different from the grievances of the Palestinians, or the Chechens, or the Kashmiris; to portray the conflicts between Muslims and the Western world as part of a cosmic battle between the forces of Truth and Falsehood, Belief and Unbelief, Good and Evil that all Muslims, Jews, and Christians—three faith communities with long and deeply ingrained traditions of cosmic warfare—must join.

"We are at war," Mohammed Saddique Khan concluded in his suicide video, calmly and with the unburdened conscience of a man whose every consideration rests on a cosmic plane. *"And I am a soldier."*

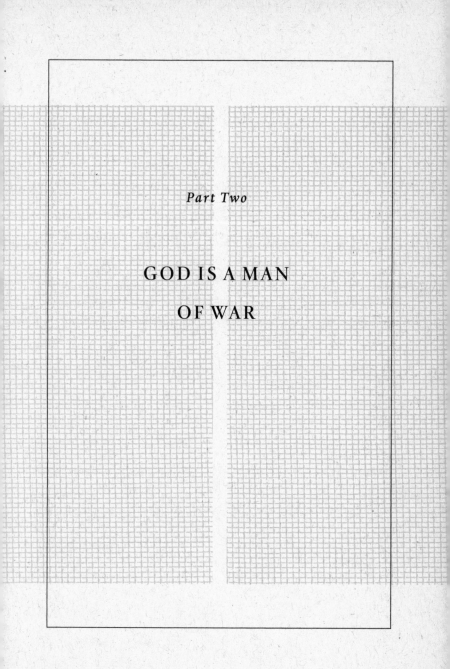

*Part Two*

# GOD IS A MAN
# OF WAR

# CHAPTER THREE

# Zeal for Your House
# Consumes Me

It was a casual, almost offhand remark; unscripted, though hardly inadvertent—not from a politician for whom public professions of faith had become a kind of verbal tic, a president whose most prosaic speeches were peppered with biblical allusions. It was the spontaneity of the remark, which, James Carroll noted, "came to him as naturally as a baseball reference," that caused such a jolt. It was as though the world, having waited four anxious days for America's response to the most heinous violation of its shores in half a century, was able to peel back the curtain of counselors and coaches who directed the president's every move and, for a brief, fleeting moment, peer into the mind of the man himself.

I caught the statement on television and recognized immediately, along with millions of Americans and hundreds of millions around the globe, that the new century had just been branded for a generation or more.

"This crusade," President Bush said, pausing for what seemed like an eternity. "This war on terrorism." Pause. "Is going to take a while."

*Crusade.*

The word hung in the air like an undetonated bomb, long enough for its myriad implications to come to mind; long enough, surely, for that one most devastating inference to be fully absorbed.

**Cru•sade** (*noun*): One of a series of medieval wars of religion waged by Christians against Muslims.

"Crusade" means "holy war"; it was the Crusades that originated the term. This is no simple word but an emblem for an era when the cross of Christ was brandished as a sword by one barbaric, theocratic empire against another barbaric, theocratic empire. As Carroll notes, the Crusades were not just a series of military campaigns, they were the defining event that shaped "a cohesive western identity precisely in opposition to Islam, an opposition that survives to this day."

No doubt this is how a great many Americans—already brimming with religious fury—understood the term, as did a large swath of the Arab and Muslim world, which had been feeling edgy and discomfited by President Bush's overt evangelical worldview ever since he had taken office. It certainly did not help matters that "Crusades" is rendered into Arabic as *hurub as-salib*—"The Wars of the Cross"—which is how the Arab press reported Bush's statement: "this war of the cross . . . this war on terrorism . . ."

True, President Bush made a hasty about-face, going out of his way in the following weeks to assure Muslims around the world that he had no intention of launching a campaign against Islam. "The enemy of America is not our many Muslim friends," he declared, as his advisers stumbled over one another to explain that the word he had used was not meant in its historical sense. This was "crusade" with a lowercase *c:* an aggressive campaign against an idea or a movement, as in "a crusade against evildoers."

But even as I accepted these excuses and explanations, I recognized how futile they were, not because I was incapable of forgiving a flub but because in that first, intuitive reaction to the attacks of September

11, 2001, the man to whom the whole of the world was looking to provide meaning and context to what had happened (and what would happen in response) had, in a sudden, involuntary stumble, set the tone for the first great conflict of the new century. At the very least, Bush had ensured that henceforth "this war on terrorism," which at that point had yet to be defined by anyone, would become synonymous with "this crusade." In doing so, he not only gave Americans an apocalyptic lens through which to view the coming conflict with the Muslim world (though, in truth, many Americans needed no encouragement), he responded with precisely the cosmic dualism that those who carried out the attacks had intended to provoke. As bin Laden gleefully declared to a reporter a few days after the president's comment, "Our goal is for our Muslim community to unite in the face of the Christian Crusade . . . Bush said it himself: *Crusade* . . . People make apologies for him; they say he didn't mean to say that this was a Crusader war, even though he himself said it was!"

"The odd thing about this," bin Laden continued, "is that he has taken the words right out of our mouths."

The Crusades have long loomed large in the Arab imagination, though, interestingly, not until some eight hundred years after they began, during the colonial era, when the image of cross-marked knights riding out to cleanse the Holy Land of heathen Muslim hordes became the most potent symbol of the imperialist aspirations of the West: a kind of shorthand for Christian aggression against Islam. "The Crusader spirit runs in the blood of all Westerners," wrote Sayyid Qutb, the twentieth century's most influential Islamist thinker.

The connection between crusade and colonialism—and, more broadly, between Christianity and Western imperialism—has since been etched into the Arab psyche. In many Muslim majority states, it is still the principal frame of reference through which relations with Europe and North America are viewed. When, in September 2005, the Danish newspaper *Morgenavisen Jyllands-Posten* published a series of offensive caricatures of the Prophet Muhammad—Muhammad wearing a bomb for a turban; Muhammad standing before two cowering, veiled women, brandishing a curved sword—leading to angry protests across Europe, a Muslim cartoonist responded with a caricature of his own: a Crusader knight, his breastplate emblazoned with Denmark's national flag (a blood-red cross), perched on an armored horse, brandishing a pencil as a lance.

For Jihadists, the Crusades are not so much a historical event as they are an ideological construct—an enduring narrative whose final chapter is only now being written in the battlefields of Afghanistan and Iraq, except it is no longer Europe but America that, as the locus of Christian imperialism in the twenty-first century, has "taken up the cross" in the eternal cosmic battle between Christianity and Islam. "This battle is not between al-Qa'ida and the U.S.," bin Laden announced in October 2001. "This is a battle of Muslims against the global Crusaders."

Such polarizing rhetoric is not easy to dismiss. Much as the Crusades helped transform a fragmented Europe into a single *corpus christianum* by redirecting the violence of Europe's warring princes toward a common foe, so do they now provide a fractured Muslim world with a symbol of unity and defiance against foreign aggression, both real and imagined. "Bush said, 'Either you are with us, or you are with terrorism,'" bin Laden exclaimed. "[I say] either you are with the Crusade, or you are with Islam."

The Crusades were the quintessential expression of cosmic war: a divine conflict thought to be taking place simultaneously on earth and in the heavens. On a purely material level, the Crusades functioned first and foremost as an expression of papal authority over external (Jews, Muslims) and internal (heterodox Christians, disobedient princes) enemies of the Church. The intricate web of papal indulgences, donations, subsidies, and taxes that funded the entire crusading enterprise—"the practical business of the cross," as one historian calls it—created a wholly new financial relationship between the Church and the royals by centralizing wealth and military power in the hands of the pope. Those who took part in the campaigns were offered not only forgiveness of sins but also forgiveness of debts, immunity from prosecution, even promises of booty seized from Muslim lands.

At the same time, the Crusades were consciously conceived of as a new means of earning salvation from the Church. This was war as an act of piety; its purpose, as spelled out by Pope Urban II in 1095 during the Council of Clermont, the ecclesiastical gathering that initiated the First Crusade, was to grant forgiveness of sins to those who would fight against the Church's enemies. "I, or rather the Lord, beseech you as Christ's heralds . . . to destroy that vile race [the Muslims] from the lands of our friends," Urban demanded of the priests, knights, and princes gathered in the small French town. "All who die by the way, whether by land or by sea, or in battle against the pagans, shall have immediate remission of sins. This I grant them through the power of God with which I am invested."

Urban was not the first pope to offer salvation to those who fought on behalf of the Church; similar promises had been made by Popes Leo IV and John VIII two hundred years earlier. In fact, the Crusades were part of a long and steady process of Christian militarization that had begun with the conversion of the Emperor Constantine around 313 C.E. Almost overnight, the provincial religion inspired by an itinerent Jew from the Galilee became an imperial religion, and the cross of Christ was turned into a banner of war. This sudden transformation radically altered the perception of Christians when it came to the notion of war and violence. The early followers of Jesus, living in a state of constant persecution and political weakness, had focused their ideas of war on the apocalyptic plane—Christ would one day return as "a warrior on a white horse," his eyes "like a flame of fire," his vestments "dripping with blood," his tongue "a sharp-edged sword" with which he would "strike down the nations" with vengeance (Revelation 19:11–15). But with the merging of Rome and Christianity, the Church's spiritual enemies became indistinguishable from Rome's political enemies. By the time the first Crusaders breached the walls of Jerusalem in 1099, four years after Urban had dispatched them to liberate the Holy Land, Christianity was no longer the secret Jewish sect whose members,

along with the rest of the Jews, had been forced out of the Holy Land
by Rome a thousand years before. It *was* Rome: rich, mighty, thirsty for
blood. The chronicles of Raymond of Agiles, who rode with the
knights of God during the First Crusade, bear witness to the almost
unimaginable violence unleashed upon the inhabitants of Jerusalem:
the Crusaders cut off the heads of Muslims and Jews, shot them with
arrows, tortured them by casting them into fires. Piles of heads, hands,
and feet littered the cobblestoned streets. The Crusaders rode in blood
up to their bridle reins, slashing their way through the bodies of the
dead—men, women, and children—until they arrived at the Temple
Mount, which they soaked in blood. "This day," declared an exultant
Raymond, "marks the justification of all Christianity and the humiliation of paganism; our faith is renewed."

It may be difficult to reconcile the unrestrained bloodlust of these
Medieval Christian soldiers with Jesus's commandments to "love one's
enemies" and "turn the other cheek." But that is because Christianity's
conception of cosmic war is derived not from the New Testament but
from the Hebrew Bible (Old Testament). The knights who raped and
pillaged their way to the Holy Land, who, in the words of the Christian
chronicler Radulph of Caen, "boiled pagan adults whole in cooking
pots, impaled children on spits and devoured them grilled," were cosmic warriors walking in the path of the Lion of Judah, not the Lamb
of God.

The concept of cosmic war, which in its simplest expression refers to
the belief that God is actively engaged in human conflicts on behalf of
one side against the other, is deeply ingrained in the Hebrew Bible.
"God is a Man of War," the Bible says (Exod. 15:3). He "goes forth like
a soldier, like a warrior he stirs up his fury; he cries out, he shouts
aloud, he shows himself mighty against his foes" (Isa. 42:13). He is "a
blood-splattered" God (Isa. 63:3), cruel to his rivals, fearsome with his
foes. With his "naked bow" and his "flashing spear" at his side, he rides
his war chariot to victory (Hab. 3:8–11). In a rage he "treads the earth";
in anger he "tramples the nations" (Hab. 3:12). He smashes the heads

of those who stand against him, and bids his followers "to bathe their feet in the blood of his enemies" (Ps. 68: 21–23). His anger shakes the heavens; the mountains writhe at his fury.

God, as conceived of in the ancient mind, was not a passive force in war but an active soldier. Central to biblical ideas about cosmic war was the belief that it is not human beings who fight on behalf of God, but rather God who fights on behalf of human beings. Sometimes God is the only warrior on the battlefield. When the Babylonians conquered Mesopotamia, they did so not in the name of their king but in the name of their god, Marduk, who was believed to have sanctioned, initiated, and commanded each battle. The same holds true for the Egyptians and their god Amun-Re; the Assyrians and their god, Ashur; the Canaanites and their god, Baal; and, most especially, the Israelites and their god, Yahweh.

Throughout the Bible, God is frequently presented as fighting on behalf of the Israelites, whose size and strength in battle are meaningless. "Nothing can hinder the Lord from saving by many or by few" (1 Sam. 14:6). Often, all the Israelites need do is stand back and believe. Behold Moses, unwavering on the banks of the Sea of Reeds, Pharaoh's chariots racing toward him: "Do not be afraid, stand firm, and see the deliverance that the Lord will accomplish for you today," Moses exhorts the trembling Israelites. "The Lord will fight for you, *and you have only to keep still.*" With a wave of his staff, the waters are driven back and the sea made dry as land. Even the Egyptians recognize the presence of Israel's God on the battlefield. "Let us flee from the Israelites," they cry, "for the Lord is fighting for them against Egypt."

It is too late. Another wave of the staff and the sea returns to its flow. The whole of Pharaoh's army is drowned. "Thus the Lord saved Israel that day from the Egyptians; and Israel saw the Egyptians dead on the seashore" (Ex. 14:30–31).

God's divine intervention in battle can take many forms, from direct action—as when the Lord hurls "huge stones from heaven" upon the fleeing men of Gibeon so that "there were more who died because of the hailstones than the Israelites killed with the sword" (Josh.

10:11)—to the excitation of nature: the creation of hail, wind, or sand-storms; the spreading of famine or disease among the enemy.

Regardless of the form of intervention, what matters is the belief that God is actively present in the battle. God "travels along with Israel's camp" (Deut. 23:14). He marches with his armies, personally commanding the forces on the ground, making strategic decisions as the fight rages around him. "Shall I go up against the Philistines?" David, the king of Israel, inquired of the Lord. "You shall not go up," the Lord replied. "Go around to their rear, and come upon them opposite the balsam trees" (2 Sam. 5:19, 23).

The battle is God's battle, the enemy is God's enemy, the strategy is God's strategy, the victory is God's victory. Indeed, when it comes to war, there is little room in the Bible for human notions of justice and morality. Whatever God decrees is ethical and right. The only limits are God's limits. "Now go and attack the Amalekites," God orders Saul, Israel's incipient king, "and utterly destroy all that they have; do not spare them, but kill both man and woman, child and infant, ox and sheep, camel and donkey" (1 Sam. 15:3).

This act of "utter annihilation" (*herem,* in Hebrew), in which God commands the wholesale slaughter of "all that breathes," is a recurring theme in the Bible. The Israelites thought of idolatry (the worship of foreign gods) as a virus that contaminated everything around it. Mere separation from the gods of foreign tribes was not enough to ensure purity. To truly rid the land of the idolatrous force and ensure the exclusive worship of Israel's god, neighboring tribes had to be eradicated. "Anyone who sacrifices to any god but Yahweh shall be utterly destroyed" (Exod. 22:20). Yet even that was not enough to contain the virus. The enemy's land, livestock, farms and fields, gold and silver had also to be destroyed, "lest they make you sin against me," says the Lord (Exod. 23:33).

Hence the tale of the hapless Achan, narrated in the book of Joshua. After the fall of Jericho, when Israel had "devoted to destruction all in the city, both men and women, young and old, oxen, sheep, and donkeys" (Josh. 6:21), Achan secretly ferreted away some of the city's loot for himself, burying it beneath his home. When discovered, Achan was not only forced to return the objects so that they could be destroyed, he himself, having been contaminated by the idolatrous force, was stoned to death, along with his wife, his children, and his children's children. Their corpses, and all of Achan's property and live-stock, were dumped on a pyre and set on fire (Josh. 7:16–26).

Obviously, when confronting any biblical text, one must remember that these are not descriptions of historical events but rather theological reflections of events long since past. Archaeological evidence suggests that some of the tribes the Israelites claimed to have annihilated were actually absorbed into their nation. But the biblical ideal of cosmic war is exceedingly clear. It is "ethnic cleansing as a means of ensuring cultic purity," to quote the great biblical scholar John Collins. It was, in fact, the principal means through which the nation was made. Follow the trail of blood left behind by Joshua's armies as he systematically rid the Promised Land of foreigners:

Joshua took Makkedah, he utterly destroyed every person in it, he left none remaining; Then Joshua, and all Israel with him, passed on to Libnah, and struck it with the edge of his sword, and every person in it, he left none remaining; Next Joshua passed on to Lachish, and struck it with the edge of his sword, and every person in it. From Lachish Joshua passed on to Eglon, and every person in it he utterly destroyed, as he had done to Lachish; Then Joshua went up from Eglon to Hebron, he left none remaining; Then Joshua turned back to Debir, and all Israel with him, and utterly destroyed every person in it, he left none remaining; Thus Joshua defeated the whole land, the hill country and the Negeb, the lowland and the slopes, he left none remaining, but utterly destroyed all that breathed, *as the Lord God of Israel had commanded,* because the Lord God of Israel fought for Israel (Josh. 10:28–42).

———

As we shall see, the biblical conception of cosmic war as an act of utter annihilation still lingers in the imaginations of a few radical, right-wing Jewish groups in modern-day Israel that hold fast to God's command to cleanse the Holy Land of all "foreign" elements, no matter the cost. But at the turn of the first millennium C.E., in the turbulent landscape of first-century Palestine,* one group of religious nationalists pushed the biblical doctrine of cosmic war to its ghastly extreme. They were known as the Zealots.

The Zealots were not a formal religious group or political party. They were a loosely affiliated, heterogeneous movement of Jewish revolutionaries, centered in the Galilee—long a hotbed of radicals and rabble-rousers—who shared contempt for the Roman occupation of Jerusalem and a fierce opposition to the Temple authorities. Some Zealots were members of the priestly class; others raged against the priesthood. Some practiced prophecy and soothsaying, while others seemed wholly detached from all aspects of the Jewish religion. A few Zealots were pacifists, but the great majority believed in the unflinching use of violence against both the Roman occupiers and those Jews they termed "collaborators." A great many Zealots were little more than roaming bands of outlaws and bandits. Yet despite their differences, what united all of these brigands and revolutionaries under the mantle of "Zealot" was an appeal to the biblical doctrine of zeal.

Best defined as "jealous anger," biblical zeal implies an unwavering commitment to God's rule, an uncompromising fidelity to God's law, and, most crucially, the complete separation of God's people from their neighbors. It is in the divine character of God that the doctrine of zeal finds its inspiration. "The Lord your God is a devouring fire, a jealous God," the Bible says (Deut. 4:24). This is a God who tolerates no equal, abides no partner, accepts no portion but the whole. He de-

---

*In the Roman era, Palestine was the name given to the vast tract of land encompassing all of modern-day Israel/Palestine as well as large parts of Jordan, Syria, and Lebanon. At this time, "Israel" referred specifically to the Northern Tribes of Israelites (the south was called Judah) and collectively to the community of Jews living in Palestine.

mands absolute and unqualified devotion and reacts with uninhibited rage when receiving anything less. To worship the God of Israel with zeal is to burn with a similar, all-consuming jealousy—for his word, his law, and his eternal rule, on earth and in heaven.

The most celebrated model of biblical zeal is Phinehas, the grandson of Aaron (Moses' brother). In those days, a plague festered among the Israelites as God's anger burned against his Chosen People. In direct violation of God's law, the Jews had been engaging in sexual acts with neighboring Moabite women, and even sacrificing to Moabite gods. In a jealous fit, God instructs Moses, as leader of the community, to take all the Jews who had violated their sexual purity and "impale them in the sun before the Lord, in order that the fierce anger of the Lord may turn away from Israel" (Num. 25:4). But before Moses can follow through on God's command, the young Phinehas decides to take up God's call, on his own and without guidance.

Phinehas spies a Jew named Zimri leading a Moabite woman into his tent. He follows them inside, where, in an act of personal zeal, he thrusts his spear into their copulating bodies. All at once, the plague is lifted. "Phinehas son of Eleazar, son of Aaron the priest, has turned back my wrath from the Israelites," God informs Moses, "by manifesting such zeal among them on my behalf that in my jealousy I did not consume the Israelites" (Num. 25:11). Far from being punished for the murder of a fellow Jew, Phineas is rewarded by God with "a covenant of peace." Henceforth, he and his family will be granted perpetual priesthood, "because he was zealous for his God" (Num. 25:13).

Phinehas's example of spontaneous, individual action as an expression of God's jealous anger and as atonement for the sins of the Jewish nation became the model of personal righteousness in the Bible. When Elijah slaughtered the priests of God's Canaanite rival, Baal, he did so because he was "zealous for the Lord" (1 Kings 19:10). When King Jehu massacred every inhabitant of Samaria, it too was to demonstrate his "zeal for the Lord" (2 Kings 10:15–17). Most pious Jews in the first century C.E. revered these biblical heroes and strove to emulate their zeal, each in his or her own way. But for the Zealots, zeal was more than just a doctrine. It was a symbol of collective identity and a call to collective action.

The origins of the Zealot movement can be traced to the year 6 C.E., when Rome called for a census to be taken of all of Syria and Palestine. It was customary for the Romans to conduct periodic registers of their citizens, along with their wives, children, slaves, and property, for the purpose of proper taxation. But this time, a small band of Jewish reactionaries from the Galilee decided to take a stand: They would not be counted. The land was not Rome's to be parceled out and tallied. The land was God's, and only God could claim ownership of it. To cooperate with the Roman census would be to acknowledge Rome's dominion, and that would be an act of sacrilege: a violation of the first and greatest commandment, revealed to Moses on Mount Sinai, to take no other god besides Yahweh (Exod. 20:3). Any Jew who deigned to be registered by Rome was in effect swearing allegiance to Rome instead of to God and was thus no longer a Jew. He was an apostate; he would be slated for death.

At first, these reactionaries congregated around a charismatic rabbi named Judas the Galilean, who, along with an obscure Pharisee named Zaddok (or Saddok), founded a new sect of Judaism that the first-century historian Flavius Josephus called the Fourth Philosophy (the first three philosophies being the Pharisees, the Sadducees, and the Essenes). This sect—perhaps faction is a more accurate designation—distinguished itself from all other religio-political groups in first-century Palestine by focusing on a single, all-encompassing ideology: the sole rule of God. Members of the Fourth Philosophy pledged to serve no lord save the One Lord. God was their King, and his Kingdom, though enthroned in Jerusalem, encompassed the whole of the world.

This was not some future kingdom to be established at the end of time. The future was already here; God's Kingdom had already arrived. All that was needed was to acknowledge this fact and begin acting upon it, which required not only the rejection of all earthly authorities but, as the Hebrew Bible demands, the removal of all gen-

tiles, foreigners, and apostate Jews from the Promised Land: purifica-
tion through destruction, just as the Lord had commanded when the
Israelites had first set foot upon the Holy Land five hundred years earlier. Only when the Jews refused to be slaves to Rome could they right-
fully call God their master. Only when the land was cleansed of
foreigners would God's reign on earth be realized. Redemption was at
hand. A decision had to be made: to be with God or with Rome. There
was no middle ground.

To emphasize their unconditional commitment to the sovereignty
of God, the members of the Fourth Philosophy would not use or even
touch a coin on which the image of Caesar was engraved. They would
not walk through gates upon which were perched statues of Roman
gods. They would touch no one outside of their group, and if they did,
they cleansed themselves immediately. If they came upon an uncir-
cumcised Jew, they would forcibly circumcise him; if they heard a Jew
call anyone Lord except God, they would kill him on the spot.

Although it is unclear whether members of the Fourth Philosophy
referred to themselves as Zealots, there is no doubt that they were the
first revolutionary movement in Palestine to use the doctrine of zeal to
unite the various economic, political, and religious grievances of the
Jews for a single aim: the establishment of the rule of God. Zeal provided a familiar symbol, recognized by all Jews, around which a new
collective identity could be formed—an identity beyond the control of
the Temple authorities. Adherence to zeal set the members of the
Fourth Philosophy apart from all other Jews in Palestine, whose acqui-
escence to Rome made them collaborators at best, apostates at worst.
The example of the Bible's zealous heroes became a sanction for the
use of violence. Indeed, zeal in the name of God demanded violence,
for it was the sacred duty of the Jews to maintain the purity of the land.

Convinced that God would reward their zeal, Judas and his tiny
band of followers launched a reckless and ill-considered revolt against
Rome. They knew that victory over the Roman empire was impossible, but they never wavered from their belief that, in Josephus's words,
"God would more surely assist them in their undertaking, if, inspired

by such ideals, they spared no effort to realize them." In any case, they were not concerned with victory. They were merely following God's will.

It was a short-lived revolution. Judas's rag-tag army was easily annihilated by the Roman legions, and Judas himself was killed in battle. His followers were captured and crucified en masse on the outskirts of the city—crucifixion being the standard Roman punishment for sedition.

But Judas the Galilean was not forgotten. Of the many charismatic revolutionaries who roamed Palestine at the turn of the first century, he is one of only a handful to be mentioned in the New Testament (Acts 5:37). By making opposition to Roman occupation a religious duty, and by being willing to resort to violence in order to bring about Israel's liberation, Judas the Galilean created a model of resistance that would be revived a generation later by a more determined group of zealous revolutionaries, who, having learned a valuable lesson from the failure of Judas's uprising, recognized that the best way to rid the Promised Land of the Roman abomination was not to attack Rome directly but to provoke Rome into attacking the Jews, thus forcing their fellow countrymen to war.

Through targeted assassinations and random acts of violence, these new, one could say *reawakened* Zealots (like their predecessors, united less by a cohesive political platform than by a shared sense of zeal for God) launched a new campaign of terror throughout Palestine. They abducted members of the Jewish aristocracy and held them for ransom. They slayed both Roman officials and Temple priests in broad daylight, on feast days and holidays, in markets and temples, in the midst of great crowds. Their main purpose seems to have been to prove that they could strike at will, that no one was safe. "More terrible than the crimes themselves was the fear they aroused, every man hourly expecting death, as in war," Josephus wrote. Some even fomented Jewish pogroms in an attempt to create a siege mentality among the Jews, to convince them that war with Rome was inevitable, that it was *decreed*.

And yet, despite the murder and mayhem they unleashed upon Palestine, these pious revolutionaries remained enormously popular, particularly among the young. This was not a peasants' revolt. The Zealots and their compatriots enjoyed widespread support among all classes in Palestine. Their leaders were urban intellectuals who longed for social transformation. A considerable number came from respectable families, and a few seem to have held important positions in society. These weren't thugs or brutes; they were among the best and brightest of Jewish society.

What made the revolutionaries so popular and admired was not their opposition to Roman rule (a sentiment shared by practically every Jew in first-century Palestine) but rather how blatantly their uncompromising beliefs threw into relief the hypocrisy of the Temple priests. The priests acquiesced to Rome and sacrificed to its gods. The Zealots, when captured, would undergo the most gruesome torture and yet not deny God's sovereignty. The Temple priests presided over a complex infrastructure of tithes and taxation, all to their own enrichment. The Zealots raided the Temple treasury and destroyed the logs of the moneylenders, making the collection of debts impossible and thus leveling the economic playing field in Jerusalem. The Temple priests, and in particular the High Priest, purchased their positions from Rome. Among the first actions taken by the Zealots after war with Rome had finally been declared, in 66 C.E., was to oust the entire priestly nobility from the Temple and draw lots to select who would be the High Priest. (The lot fell to an illiterate country peasant named Phanni, son of Samuel, from the village of Aphthia.) The point is that while the Temple may have had jurisdiction over the religious lives of all Jews, while it may have had sole authority to define the meaning and message of Judaism, it could not command the loyalties of a band of Jews whose very identity was constructed in opposition to the Temple.

Still, it would be inaccurate to think of the Zealot movement as a *religious* movement. This motley group of priests, brigands, and social revolutionaries functioned more as a primitive social movement, one focused as much on the liberation of Israel as on religious purity. Considering that most Jews in first-century Palestine would have framed their political and religious sentiments in the same language, the Zealots' call for "the sole rule of God" would have been indistinguishable from the call for freedom from Roman occupation. As Josephus wrote, "They had an invincible love of liberty, for they held God to be their only lord and master."

It took many years for the rebels to convince their fellow Jews in 66 C.E. to rise up against Rome. And though this revolt lasted longer than the revolt of Judas the Galilean (66–69 C.E.), it too was eventually quashed, and without mercy. The war fought against what the Rabbinate of the time referred to as the "Evil Kingdom" lasted all of three years.

When, in 70 C.E., the Romans recaptured Jerusalem, they razed the Temple and defiled its ashes. Anyone with ties to the rebellion was executed, down to the last child. Every Jew—including the Christian Jews—was forced out of the holy city into permanent exile. A small band of the most ardent revolutionaries escaped to the desert and hunkered down inside an impenetrable mountain fortress west of the Dead Sea called Masada. There they waited out a Roman siege for three long, agonizing years. When the Romans finally breached Masada's walls, they found everyone inside the fortress dead. The last of the rebels—husbands, wives, children, nearly one thousand souls—had committed collective suicide, taking turns killing one another with knives and swords rather than surrender to Rome. Cosmic warriors do not surrender.

Masada today is a popular tourist destination. Its austere grandeur is unlike anything else in a land of austere grandeur. From the top of its isolated, flat rock precipice, one can see for miles across the briny waters of the Dead Sea. Every year, Israeli troops from the Army, Air Force, and Sea Corps are, after basic training, marched to the top of the fortress at Masada—the place where, two millennia ago, one thousand Jewish revolutionaries took their own lives and the lives of their wives and children rather than surrender their independence—and sworn into the Israel Defense Forces with the oath "Masada shall never again fall!"

The ceremony is symbolic, nothing more. Just as the past and the present meld into one in the Holy Land, so too do the sacred and the profane. But symbols are slippery; their meanings cannot be so easily controlled. For the Israeli soldier who stands atop Masada, this majestic place may be a symbol of heroism and national independence. But for a new movement of radical ideological settlers and Jewish cosmic warriors who have revived the Zealot ideal in modern-day Israel, Masada means something else entirely.

CHAPTER FOUR

# An Army of Believers

By the time Shlomo Goren—the chief rabbi of the Israel Defense Forces and himself a war-worn and accoladed major general—reached the Old City of Jerusalem, someone (some swift-footed junior officer, perhaps) had already planted the flag of Israel atop the Dome of the Rock. It was June 7, 1967. Two days earlier, the fate of the nascent state of Israel had appeared to be sealed. Hundreds of thousands of Arab troops—the combined forces of Syria, Egypt, and Jordan—were bearing down on the tiny state. Yet here was Goren, a mere forty-eight hours later, racing through the heart of the Old City—a Torah scroll tucked under his arm, a ram's horn, or shofar, in his hand—triumphant and on his way to reclaim the Temple Mount.

The fighting had not yet ceased. There was still a determined corps of Jordanian troops maintaining positions around the Old City, firing wildly and in vain at the Israeli tanks. Bullets whizzed by Goren's head. But nothing would stop him from rushing up to the Temple—not the Israeli commander shouting for him to turn back, not the knife-sharp pang in his chest.

"The Temple Mount is ours!" he heard someone say. His heart nearly burst at the thought.

Rabbi Goren had immigrated to Palestine from Poland in 1925. His father was one of the leaders of a movement of Religious Zionists who believed that the establishment of the state of Israel would soon initiate the coming of the Messiah and the redemption of humanity. Reared in an Orthodox village near Haifa called Kfar Hasidim, Goren was a man of almost preternatural intellect. At the age of seventeen he published his first book, a dense treatise on the great Jewish philosopher Moses Maimonides titled *The Crown of Holiness*.

Maimonides believed it was the responsibility of every generation of Jews to strive to rebuild the Temple. It was the House of God, after all, the link between earth and heaven. Goren agreed, as did a growing number of young Orthodox leaders, radical settlers, and yeshiva students, who, in direct opposition to traditional Orthodox teachings, argued that it was not only permissible but mandatory for Jews to worship atop the Temple Mount—that simply praying for the Temple's restoration was not enough; one had to fight for it. And here they now were, a nation at last, *fighting for it.*

Once atop the Temple Mount, Goren took a moment to catch his breath. The view was majestic: Mount Zion to the west. To the east, the Mount of Olives. There was Hebron! And there Jericho! The land promised by God to his ancestors, *all of it,* in his sights for very the first time.

With the ram's horn pressed to his lips, Goren turned to face the Holy of Holies—now the Dome of the Rock—summoned what breath he had left, and blew. The Israeli soldiers trudging up Mount Moriah heard the call. They dashed to the top of the Temple platform and, in a sudden apocalyptic rush, enveloped the rabbi, raising him into the air as he continued to blow the clarion call announcing to all of Israel's children the retaking of the Temple Mount.

Then someone took a picture.

I have that photo, here before me. Rabbi Goren is wearing Coke-bottle glasses, but I tell you, I can see the light dancing in his eyes. With the ram's horn pressed to his lips he is Joshua, calling forth the wrath of God who crumbles mountains. He is Aaron, staring out with virgin eyes upon the land of milk and honey. He is Moses: see how the soldiers run to him through the parting of dust and rubble! Two thousand years of wandering in the wilderness, and now, at long last, Eretz Yisrael is secured. Surely redemption is at hand.

Rabbi Goren could hardly be blamed for such apocalyptic fervor. By the end of what came to be known as the Six-Day War in 1967, Israel had captured the Sinai Peninsula, the Gaza Strip, the West Bank, East Jerusalem, and the Golan Heights—the totality of biblical Israel. Its external enemies had been laid to waste, and with ease. Who could deny God's hand in the victory? For a great many Jews, Israel's war with the Arab armies was understood not in the earthly context of governments and political affairs but in the cosmic context of good fighting evil, darkness defeating light. The Jewish David had smitten the Arab Goliath. The prophecy had been fulfilled. The End of Days was at hand!

Even the most secular Israeli could not fail to be moved by the thought that the war was divine providence. Within hours of the army's taking of the Temple, bulldozers began destroying Palestinian homes in front of the Wailing Wall, making it accessible to the Jews for the first time in centuries. Within months, the first settlers, mostly Religious Zionists from Goren's own village, Kfar Hasidim, and its sister village, Kfar Etzion, began settling the West Bank. With the victory of 1967 and the occupation of Palestinian lands, Secular Zionism, once anathema to many Orthodox Jews, was gradually being framed as merely a transient stage in God's master plan for the Jewish people— a precursor to the reestablishment of the Kingdom of David.

The notion that the state of Israel was just a placeholder for the eventual rule of God was not new. It was, in fact, the core belief of Religious Zionism. The idea emerged in the teachings of a charismatic rabbi named Avraham Yitzhak HaCohen Kook (1865–1935). Rabbi Kook and his disciples thought of the state as "an external shell that would later be replaced by a messianic future, whose overt purpose was the reinstatement of the religious ritual on [the Temple Mount]."

In 1921, Rabbi Kook established an institute in Jerusalem dedicated to rebuilding the Temple. "Our faith is firm," he said, "that days are coming when all the nations shall recognize that this place, which the Lord has chosen for all eternity as the site of our Temple, must return to its true owners, and the great and holy House [the Temple] must be built thereon."

Of course, rebuilding the Temple would mean razing the Dome of the Rock. A story is told about Rabbi Goren: After blowing the ram's horn, the rabbi ran up to General Uzi Narkiss, the commander of the Israel Defense Forces, and urged him to blow up the Dome of the Rock—now, before things settled, before the politicians and the peace-makers appeared. General Narkiss brushed Goren off, and control over the Temple Mount was returned to Jerusalem's Muslim authorities. But the dream of the Religious Zionists to seize control of the Temple Mount in preparation for the coming of the Messiah never diminished.

At the heart of the Religious Zionist movement is the belief that the Jews are asleep, that they must be forcibly awakened and spurred into action. The temporary capture of the Temple Mount was the wake-up call. The Religious Zionists argued that the war of 1967 had been God's design: God had compelled the Arabs to attack Israel in order to force the Jews to fight back and thus liberate all of the Promised Land. Rabbi Kook's eldest son, Tzvi Yehuda Kook, the founder of the radical settler movement Gush Emunim (The Believers' Bloc), argued that even the Holocaust had been "a cruel divine operation in order to lift [the Jews] up to the Land of Israel against their wills."

With the call of the shofar ringing in their ears, the Religious Zionists set to work creating an unalterable reality on the ground by settling captured Palestinian lands. Settlement was never meant to be official Israeli policy—not initially. But there was little the government could do to prevent it. The state held no sovereignty over the religious beliefs of the settlers. "The wholeness of the Land of Israel is not within the realm of the government of Israel's decision," declared Ya'akov Filber, a disciple of Rabbi Tzvi Kook.

Tzvi Kook died in 1982, but his spirit lives in the settler movement he left behind. In fact, over the last three decades, Gush Emunim has transformed itself from a small band of Religious Zionists centered in and around Rabbi Goren's hometown of Kfar Hasidim into the largest and most powerful social movement in Israel, "a semi-official governing body," in the words of political scientist Ian Lustick, one whose organizational network spans the entire country. Gush Emunim has for years managed to dominate Israeli politics by insinuating its goals into the political platforms of radical religious parties like the ultra-Orthodox Shas, the Yahadut HaTorah, and the Jewish National Front party, which seeks to replace the civil law of the state with the religious law of the Torah. However, its current alignment with the right-wing Likud party, whose platform rejects the possibility of a Palestinian state and refers to the Occupied Territories by their biblical names, Judea and Samaria, now allows members of Gush Emunim to engage directly in the implementation of government policies in the Occupied Territories.

Like their Zealot predecessors, Gush Emunim and like-minded Religious Zionists insist on a state governed wholly by religious law, one in which the land is cleansed of its "foreign" inhabitants so as to hasten the return of the Messiah; non-Jews, and even secular Jews, have no place in the divine Israel imagined by the Gush. Indeed, just as zeal provided a symbol of spontaneous individual action that united the various revolutionary groups in first-century Palestine across regional, religious, and social boundaries, so now does it unite a broad coalition of Religious Zionists, ultra-Orthodox *haredim*, ideological settler groups (residents of Itamar, Rahelim, Yitzhar, Shalhevet Ya, Amona, Har Bracha, and dozens of other mostly illegal settlements dotting the West Bank), and yeshiva students, who together have formed what the French scholar of religions Gilles Kepel terms a "re-Judaization movement" in Israel. By carving out a distinct and separate collective identity for themselves that is beyond the control of both the secular

authority of the Israeli state and the religious authority of Israel's Rab-
binical Council, these modern-day Zealots are actively engaged in sup-
planting the secular Zionism that has defined Israel's political identity
since its inception with a messianic Zionism whose ultimate goal is the
dismantling of the secular state altogether.

In repeated confrontations with the Israeli army, most recently in
Israel's unilateral withdrawal from Gaza, the Religious Zionists have
shown that they would prefer civil war in Israel to peace with the Palestinians. That is because these Jews define their national identity in
terms not of civic loyalty to the *state* but of religious obligation to the
*land*. For them the state of Israel has no intrinsic value, other than to
serve as a vehicle for the settlement of Jews. Their national narrative
begins not with Dreyfus and Herzl but with Moses and Aaron. Their
divine mission is to ensure that the Occupied Territories are permanently annexed into the state of Israel, that not one inch of God's
promised land will ever be returned to the Palestinians. And as they
have repeatedly demonstrated, they will go to any length to disrupt
peace negotiations that may lead to a Palestinian state, even if it means
killing their fellow Jews. Thus, the homes of Israelis who have criti-
cized illegal settlements have been bombed, and fliers have been distributed in Jerusalem offering hundreds of thousands of dollars to
anyone who kills a member of the Israeli advocacy group Peace Now,
which favors dismantling the settlements as part of a peace plan with
the Palestinians. As a settler leader told *The New York Times* in 2008, the
Jews must decide "whether they are on the side of the Torah or the
state."

It was one of these Jewish radicals, Yigal Amir, who assassinated Israeli Prime Minister Yitzhak Rabin after he had signed the Oslo Peace
Accords, which promised to return lands seized in 1967 to the Palestinians as a first step toward a lasting peace. Amir's actions almost
single-handedly derailed the peace process and put an end to the Oslo
Accords—just as he had intended. Asked why he would commit such a
heinous crime and under whose orders, Yigal Amir replied that he had
acted alone and without guidance from anyone save God—just like

Phinehas. His actions, he argued, had been justified both by Jewish law and by precedent. "According to the Halacha [Jewish law] you can kill the enemy," he told the magistrate at his trial. "My whole life, I learned Halacha. When you kill in war, it is an act that is allowed." It was quite simple, really: Rabin was giving away God's land in return for peace. He had therefore forfeited his identity as a Jew. He was now "the enemy," a traitor, an apostate. His sin was a blight upon the whole of the land; it had to be wiped away. By killing Rabin, Amir believed, he was saving Israel from God's judgment. He was, according to his wife, sacrificing himself for the sake of God's people.

Yigal Amir has been branded a zealot, a radical, a terrorist, even a madman. But the truth is that his views on the sanctity and inviolability of biblical Israel, and the measures that could be taken according to Jewish law to cleanse and preserve the totality of the Promised Land, are surprisingly widespread in modern-day Israel. A 2006 poll conducted by the Dahaf Institute for the Israeli newspaper *Yedioth Ahronoth* revealed that nearly a third of Israelis favored pardoning Amir for Rabin's assassination. Among self-described "religious" Israelis, support for Amir's release reached 50 percent. In 2007, on the thirteenth anniversary of Rabin's murder, a packed soccer stadium in Haifa erupted in chants of "Yigal Amir! Yigal Amir!" when the announcer asked for a moment of silence to honor the former prime minister.

It is not only in Israel that one finds support for men like Amir and his fellow Jewish cosmic warriors. When Pat Robertson, America's premier evangelical preacher, heard about the assassination of Yitzhak Rabin, he was convinced it was part of God's master plan for the region. "This is God's land," Robertson declared, "and God has strong words about someone who parts and divides His land. The rabbis put a curse on Yitzhak Rabin when he began cutting up the land."

Robertson is not just an evangelical media mogul. He is one of the principal figures in a coalition of evangelical organizations, based mostly in the United States, dedicated to helping Israel's cosmic warriors maintain their grasp on the whole of the land. These so-called

Christian Zionists (the term was coined by Theodor Herzl to refer to the Christian colonialists who supported the creation of the state of Israel) are motivated by the conviction that the politics of Israel, and indeed of the entire Middle East, are being orchestrated by God. And like their Jewish and Muslim counterparts in Israel and Palestine, they are actively engaged in working against the peace process, which, they argue, is "an international plot to steal Jerusalem from the Jews"— a plot that, in the words of the evangelical writer Mike Evans, is being controlled by "a master collaborator [Satan] who is directing the play." As the megachurch pastor John Hagee, the high priest of Christian Zionism, has proudly declared, "God doesn't care what the United Nations thinks. He gave Jerusalem to the nation of Israel, and it is theirs."

Like Israel's Jewish cosmic warriors, these Christian cosmic warriors believe that the Jews must rebuild the Temple in Jerusalem in order to usher in the return of the Messiah. Of course, as Christians, they believe that the Messiah is Jesus Christ and that when he returns to earth the Jews will have to either convert to Christianity or be damned. But remarkably, the last act of this cosmic drama seems not to matter much to either the Jews or the Christians in this messianic coalition. That is because what binds these two very different religious communities together under a single, transnational, collective identity is not a shared theology but a common cosmic worldview and, more important, a common cosmic foe. "The line between the political and the biblical is disappearing," explained Josh Reinstein, the director of the Israeli Parliament's Christian Allies Caucus, whose purpose is to create a covenantal relationship between Israel's Religious Zionists and America's evangelical Christians. "Around the world, we see the rise of radical Islam come against our Judeo-Christian values, and we must meet it with a well organized response." Islam is a cosmic enemy that, as the evangelical writer Hal Lindsey, the author of the apocalyptic blockbuster *The Late Great Planet Earth*, has written, "seeks not only to destroy the state of Israel, but also the overthrow of the Judeo-Christian civilization—the very foundation of our western civilization." For Lindsey and his fellow Christian cosmic warriors, the conflict between Israel and Palestine is not a political problem to be diplomatically resolved but "Ground Zero in the end time events." In their imagination, the armies of Good and Evil are already gathering in the Holy Land in preparation for that final battle, when this valley of gently sloping hills and gnarled olive groves will be filled with the machines of war, with blood, and with the bodies of the fallen.

Yet while these Christian Zionists believe that the final battle on earth will begin in Jerusalem, the attacks of 9/11 and the resulting War on Terror have, in their minds, expanded the theater of conflict and shifted the epicenter of the cosmic war to what they like to call "God's New Israel": America. Americans have always had a sense of divine destiny. The Puritans who settled this untamed land were convinced they were reliving the story of the Exodus in the New World. "We Americans are the peculiar, chosen people," Herman Melville wrote, "the Israel of our time." Jonathan Edwards, the eighteenth-century fire-and-brimstone preacher best known for his phlegmatic sermon "Sinners in the Hand of an Angry God," liked to describe America as "the new Canaan," declaring that "America has received the true religion of the old continent."

The Founding Fathers consciously conceived of the United States as "the Israel on the Potomac": a light onto the nations; a city on a hill. When asked to draft a seal to represent the new nation, Benjamin Franklin, Thomas Jefferson, and John Adams drew up a seal that depicted Moses on the shores of the Sea of Reeds, his staff raised, the waters surging over Pharaoh's army. The motto: "Rebellion to tyrants is obedience to God."

That is not to say that the United States was founded as "a Christian nation." This is a modern fantasy constructed primarily upon the pseudo historical musings of the Calvinist theologian Rousas John Rushdoony, whose best-selling books *The Messianic Character of American Education* and *Intellectual Schizophrenia* launched the Christian nationalist movement in the 1960s. Yet in throwing off the yoke of an institutional church, the new nation gradually developed into a kind of church itself. Patriotism became a form of religious devotion. The flag was transformed into a totem. The Declaration of Independence was cast as a covenant between God and his new chosen people. The Constitution took on the patina of divine scripture.

From Manifest Destiny to the War on Terror, the American experience has always been infused with a sense of sacred purpose, a conviction that America's values are God's values, meant for the whole of the world. If, after all, the principles upon which the country is founded are not just universal but *self-evident*, granted by God to all men yet established in only one nation, then it must be the task of that nation to deliver those principles to all other nations; to, in effect, carry out God's will on earth—by force if necessary. "America," preached the nineteenth-century Congregational minister Lyman Beecher, "is destined to lead the way in the moral and political emancipation of the world."

Belief in America's divine providence was not solely a Christian sentiment. As wave after wave of immigrants of all faiths and religious traditions began arriving in the New World, they too gradually adopted the notion that the United States was, in the words of Rabbi Isaac Mayer Wise, the Austrian Jewish immigrant who helped found Hebrew Union College in 1875, "now and forever the palladium of liberty and its divinely appointed banner-bearer, for the progress and redemption of mankind."

There is, of course, an obvious corollary to the idea of America's divine purpose and national righteousness. If America is the agent of God, then America's enemies—whether internal or external—must be the agents of Satan. This cosmic duality has served American politicians well, particularly in times of conflict and war. During World War I, the Committee on Public Information was tasked by the U.S. government with convincing Americans that the war was being waged "by the saints against unmitigated evil" and that the "Huns"—by which the Committee meant the Germans—"were the very creatures of Satan, completely devoid of human compassion and totally committed to wrecking the free world." Similar themes drove the propaganda of the Second World War, which Franklin Delano Roosevelt expressly painted as a battle between the cosmic forces of good and evil. "The world is too small to provide adequate 'living room,' for both Hitler and God," Roosevelt defiantly announced to Congress on January 6, 1942.

The half-century Cold War that followed World War II effectively shifted this cosmic duality onto an ideological plane, wherein the conflict was not so much between God and Satan as between God and godlessness. When Ronald Reagan, who regularly invited evangelical ideologues such as Hal Lindsey, Jerry Falwell, and Mike Evans to the White House to tutor him on scripture and prophecy, first labeled the Soviet Union "The Evil Empire" in a speech to the National Association of Evangelicals, he was using coded language that his Christian audience would have implicitly understood. Reagan was not decrying any particular Soviet action as evil. This was evil as a metaphysical force: nameless, primal, omnipresent. The opposite of good. The opposite of *us*.

Such brazen use of Christian rhetoric in support of war is, as we have seen, a legacy of the Crusades, which not only solidified the notion that physical combat against "the enemies of Christ" could be a valid expression of Christian faith but altered the very language of Christianity. The appearance on the battlefield of priests and monks, bishops, and even a pope (Leo IX), as well as members of religious military orders such as the Templars and the Hospitalers—all of them armed with "the cross of Christ"—permanently embedded into the Christian religion metaphors of war and militancy that to this day can be heard in churches around the globe, where the faithful are encouraged to "put on the armor of God" and "carry the banner of Christ into battle" and where the most mundane activities are saturated with martial imagery.

"The Christian home is to be in a constant state of war," says Ted Haggard, the disgraced former pastor of one of America's largest and most politically influential evangelical megachurches, New Life Church in Colorado Springs.

"The local church is an organized army equipped for battle, ready to charge the enemy," declared the late Jerry Falwell, the man most responsible for the meteoric rise of the Religious Right in America. "The Sunday school is the attacking squad," Falwell continued, and the task of the Christian missionary is to "bombard our territory, to move out near the coast and shell the enemy . . . to set loose on the enemy's stronghold."

Again, these are merely metaphors. Just as the Israel Defense Force employs religious symbols to bolster its military agenda, the Religious Right uses the symbols of war and militancy to buoy its social agenda. For centuries, firebrand preachers have spoken of Christian faith as a battle to be waged against the demonic forces of this world.

Still, it is difficult not to notice how this kind of militant Christian rhetoric has, over the last century, become a staple of the American evangelical movement represented by its pillars, Haggard, Falwell, and Pat Robertson. Indeed, contemporary evangelicalism seems to have so utterly absorbed the notion that warfare can be a valid expression of Christian faith that, according to research done by the preeminent scholar of American evangelicalism, George Marsden, evangelicals are far more likely than other Americans to sanction and support war. This has certainly been the case when it comes to the so-called War on Terror. A survey of the twenty-four fastest-growing evangelical churches in the Pacific Northwest, conducted by James K. Wellman of the University of Washington in 2004, revealed overwhelming enthusiasm for America's campaign in Iraq: of nearly three hundred evangelical clergy and lay leaders interviewed by Wellman, only fifteen failed to express unqualified support for the war. Two years later, when approval of the war was at an all-time low in almost every other sector in American society, another survey, this one conducted by Baylor University, concluded that 60 percent of evangelicals in the United States continued to support the war in Iraq (50 percent remained convinced, despite all evidence to the contrary, that Saddam Hussein had been directly involved in the attacks of 9/11).

It is not that evangelicals advocate war in general. However, there is something in the evangelical worldview that, in contradiction to traditional Christian teachings regarding forgiveness and nonviolence, allows for far greater zeal for war, especially if the conflict is presented through a cosmic lens. (Think of the success that Ronald Reagan's "Evil Empire" or George W. Bush's "Axis of Evil" had in capturing the evangelical imagination.) To understand why this is the case requires a closer look at the roots of evangelicalism.

Evangelicalism is not so much a religious sect as it is a social movement, focusing as it does on what it considers to be the social implications of the Gospel story. More precisely, it is a coalition of diverse and highly individualistic submovements, each of which traces its theological origins to the Christian revivalist trends that dominated Protestant churches in the United Kingdom and the United States throughout much of the eighteenth and nineteenth centuries. It would be inaccurate to consider evangelicals a distinct denomination within Christianity. Rather, this is a transdenominational movement that pulls from a host of Protestant traditions—from the Methodists to the Presbyterians, the Southern Baptists to the Pentecostals.

Modern American evangelicalism grew out of another distinctly American religious movement called fundamentalism, which arose in the early twentieth century, was a period of grave uncertainty for many conservative Christians. New and unfamiliar ideas such as Darwinism and feminism were posing extraordinary challenges to traditional Christian beliefs; the scientific revolution in general seemed to make a mockery of the idea of biblical creationism. A new generation of Christian scholars, encouraged by innovative theories of literary criticism, began scrutinizing the Bible according to such novel considerations as "cultural context" and "authorial intent." Their efforts resulted in a movement of Christian liberalism that sought to reconcile traditional Christian values with new American ideals of scientific progress, cultural relativism, and religious pluralism, all of this at a time when the rapid modernization and secularization of society had led to a swift decline in church attendance, while a massive influx of

Catholic and Jewish immigrants into the United States threatened to permanently alter the face of religion in America.

Fundamentalism (the term derives from a series of Christian tracts entitled *The Fundamentals*, published between 1909 and 1915) was a means of pushing back against these new forces in American society. Originally, the term "fundamentalism" was used to describe a militantly ultraconservative wing of the American evangelical movement ("A Fundamentalist is an Evangelical who is angry about something," George Marsden wrote). Fundamentalists argued that it was not enough merely to believe in God and obey the teachings of the Gospels. One had to make a personal, confessional commitment to Jesus Christ, so that he could wash away one's sins with his "redeeming blood." Only then could one reenter the world in purity and innocence as "born again."

Fundamentalist leaders preached a radical return to the *fundamentals* of the Christian faith. Chief among these was an uncompromising belief in the infallible, inerrant, and absolutely literal nature of the Bible. Fundamentalists regarded the Bible as one sustained historical narrative—from the creation of the world to its imminent destruction—in which every single word is "God breathed," to use a biblical phrase. In other words, not only is the Bible without error, but its myths and fables must be read as historical fact.

The fundamentalist position was a departure from traditional Christianity. Although the early Christians considered the Bible's human writers to be conduits through which the word of God was revealed, they recognized that the texts themselves had nevertheless been written by men. That is why they canonized four gospels, even though the gospels often contradict one another on such sacrosanct issues as Jesus's genealogy, the events of his birth, the chronology of his life, the date and time of his death, and the circumstances surrounding his resurrection. Rather than conceal or apologize for these discrepancies, the early Christians openly acknowledged them as part of an ongoing dialogue over the meaning and significance of Jesus's words and deeds.

For fundamentalists, however, adherence to the literal and inerrant nature of the Bible was not merely a matter of dogma, it was a test of Christian loyalty, a means of differentiating themselves from other Christians. In the 1920s and '30s, fundamentalist preachers began exhorting their flocks to regain control of Christian orthodoxy and check the rampant secularization and liberalization of American society by breaking away from mainline denominations within the larger evangelical coalition. Fundamentalist groups began forming their own independent churches, often in homes and schools. To promote their cause and to combat Christian liberalism, they built large networks of voluntary organizations whose mission was to spread their uncompromising beliefs throughout the country.

But by the 1960s, thanks in part to the friendlier, more inclusive evangelicalism espoused by the tent-revival preacher Billy Graham, the term "fundamentalist" began to fall out of favor in America, though fundamentalism itself did not disappear. Instead, its rigid social ideology and militant worldview were gradually reabsorbed into mainline evangelicalism. The result was a rift in the American evangelical coalition that led to the formation of two distinct submovements: the more socially and theologically relaxed strand, represented by groups such as the National Association of Evangelicals and by Jim Wallis's social justice organization Sojourners; and the more ideologically intransigent and socially conservative strand, represented by such groups as Pat Robertson's Christian Coalition and James Dobson's Focus on the Family (scholars of religion tend to refer to the former movement as "evangelicalism" and the latter as "fundamentalist evangelicalism").

Ultimately, the term "evangelical" is a self-designation, one that, according to polls conducted by Gallup and the Princeton Religion Research Center, more than a third of all Americans apply to themselves. There are, however, a few common traits that unite this kaleidoscopic collection of Christians under a single collective identity. The first is an uncompromising adherence to a set of fundamental doctrines that include belief in the literalism and inerrancy of the Bible; emphasis on an unmediated relationship with Jesus Christ; a zealous devotion to the conversion of others; and a cosmic worldview in which, to quote George Marsden, "the universe is divided into two—the moral and the immoral, the forces of light and darkness." Though such beliefs exist in one form or another in many Christian denominations, what distinguishes the evangelical movement is the conviction that these doctrines, when adopted rigidly and as a whole, result in a kind of spiritual rebirth that separates evangelicals from all other Christians (hence the evangelical belief that salvation belongs only to those who have been "born again").

Beyond belief in these doctrines, however, what most distinguishes evangelicals as a single community of faith is their overwhelming sense of feeling under siege. This is a reactionary movement that has, from its inception, thrived on tension and conflict, not just in its interactions with the secular world but also, and perhaps more often, in its confrontations with other Christian sects and denominations (particularly Catholicism and Mormonism, neither of which is considered a valid form of Christianity in the evangelical worldview). There exists in this movement a socially constructed atmosphere of crisis, conflict, and threat derived from the perception that, as those who have been "born again," evangelicals have inherited God's covenant from Israel. They are the new chosen people, and, like the Israelites of old, they must forever be tested by God and despised by the world.

This self-imposed worldview of constant embattlement can be impervious to reality. In the United States, where there are more than one hundred million evangelicals and nearly one thousand evangelical megachurches (defined as churches with more than two thousand members), where in 2004 almost half of the Senate and a third of the members of the House of Representatives were given an approval rating of 80 to 100 percent by evangelical watch groups, and where, until recently, the president and a great many members of his cabinet and staff were practicing evangelicals, a constant lament of evangelical leaders such as Tony Perkins of the Family Research Council and Richard Land of the Southern Baptist Convention is that the rights of evangelicals are being trampled upon because, for instance, they are not allowed to have prayer in public schools or post the Ten Commandments on government property. As the sociologist Christian Smith has noted, the evangelical movement's vibrancy, its ability to sustain a distinctive religious subculture, is owed precisely to this constructed sense of siege. Without it, Smith writes, the movement would "lose its identity and purpose and grow languid and aimless."

Just as vital to the vigor of the evangelical movement in America is its fervent religious nationalism—the conviction that the United States is "a Christian nation," appointed by God to establish Christian values throughout the rest of the world. For many evangelicals, "Christianization" and "Americanization" are inseparable ideas—the cross and the flag bleed into a single national emblem. A few evangelical groups, such as WallBuilders, Battle Cry, the Coalition on Revival, the Christian Coalition, Eagle Forum, and the Family Resource Council, even talk of replacing the Constitution with the Bible and civil law with the law of God. These Christian nationalists (sometimes called "Dominionists" or "Christianists" by scholars—the latter term is meant to emphasize their startling resemblance to adherents of another form of religious nationalism: "Islamism"), seek to "redefine traditional democratic and Christian terms and concepts to fit an ideology that calls on the radical church to take political power," as Chris Hedges writes in his study of the movement, *American Fascists.*

In the cosmic worldview of American evangelicalism, the United States has been elevated to sacred status. America's national success serves as confirmation of God's blessings; America's enemies are God's enemies. Surveys have repeatedly shown that large numbers of American evangelicals believe that God actively favors the United States in international conflicts. And perhaps this fact, more than anything else, explains why evangelicals seem to be more willing than other Americans to support state-sanctioned war. In the evangelical imagination, such wars are not merely conflicts between armies and nations; they are cosmic battles between the forces of good, represented by America, and the forces of evil, represented by America's enemies. The attacks of 9/11, which according to evangelical leaders like Mike Evans was "a dress rehearsal for Armageddon," seemed only to confirm this view, even as the wars in Afghanistan and Iraq quickly took on the tenor of a cosmic conflict against demonic forces. As Charles Stanley of the Southern Baptist Convention argued, "While we do have a real enemy who seeks our destruction, we are not defenseless. We have the strength and the energy given to us by Christ Himself. Nothing is stronger than this. The same power God used to raise His Son from the grave—resurrection power—is ours."

This blending of martial and cosmic imagery to describe America's sacred status as God's favored nation is certainly not new to U.S. history, though it did reach new heights under the presidency of George W. Bush, perhaps the most forcefully religious president in recent memory. In the days and weeks following the attacks of 9/11, Bush consciously painted the conflict with Jihadism in unapologetically cosmic terms, repeatedly declaring America's intention to "rid the world of evil." For months after the launch of the War on Terror, Bush refused to call Osama bin Laden by his name, referring to him instead as "the Evil One"—a reference to Satan from the New Testament that would not have been lost on his evangelical base (nor on the Jihadists). Bush not only elevated the United States to sacred status, he made it the agent of God's "infinite justice" (the name he originally chose for the military campaign against the Taliban in Afghanistan). In fact, he went so far as to endow the United States with Christ's salvific power when, standing on the shores of Ellis Island, he declared, "America is the hope of all mankind. . . . [It is] the light that shines in the darkness; and the darkness shall not overcome it"—an allusion to Jesus from the Gospel of John (1:5). As Gregory Boyd, himself an evangelical pastor, noted in his critique of President Bush's rhetoric, "In this paradigm, what applies to Jesus ('the light of the world') can be applied to our country, and what applies to Satan ('the darkness') can be applied to whomever resists our country. We are of God; they are of the Devil. We are the light; they are the darkness. Our wars are therefore 'holy' wars."

Bush himself took on a messianic aura in the minds of some evangelicals, as Lieutenant General William G. Boykin suggested in a much-publicized speech at the Good Shepherd Church in Oregon. "Ask yourself this," Boykin asked the congregation. "Why is this man in the White House? The majority of Americans did not vote for him. Why is he there? And I tell you this morning, he's in the White House because God put him there for such a time as this. God put him there to lead not only this nation but to lead the world, in such a time as this."

General Boykin has since retired from the military, though he remains affiliated with an evangelical missionary organization called Faith Force Multiplier, whose stated mission is to "enlist, train, and empower a great army of believers for the sake of the Kingdom of God," and to "send and maintain *military missionaries* in strategic locations throughout the world" (italics mine). Faith Force Multiplier, in fact, is part of a well-coordinated and well-funded effort, under way since before 9/11, to convert members of the U.S. Armed Forces into what Boykin himself has termed "a Christian Army." This systematic evangelicalization of the armed forces has been taking place at the very highest levels of the U.S. military; indeed, right inside the Pentagon, where another influential evangelical organization, the Christian Embassy, has become so deeply entrenched that it has been referred to as "a quasi-federal entity" by members of the military's top brass. As Army Brigadier General Robert Caslen boasted when he appeared in a promotional video for the group, the Christian Embassy is "the aroma of Jesus Christ here in the Pentagon."

The mission of the Christian Embassy is simple: convert high-ranking diplomats and military officers to evangelical Christianity so that they can then press the evangelical gospel upon their subordinates, both in the United States and abroad. The strategy is working. In the last few years, news reports, watchdog groups, and even an internal military investigation have uncovered numerous instances of overt and aggressive proselytizing by evangelical officers and faculty members at military bases and service academies across the United States. The most glaring transgressions have taken place at the U.S. Air

Force Academy in Colorado Springs, Colorado, a city hailed as the Vatican of the fundamentalist evangelical movement. Colorado Springs is home to Ted Haggard's New Life Church and James Dobson's Focus on the Family, both of which maintain close ties with the academy, offering cadets Sunday services and Bible study workshops. The city is also home to the missionary organization Campus Crusade for Christ, whose director, Scott Blom, has publicly declared his organization's intention to turn cadets at the Air Force Academy into "government-paid missionaries."

In 2006, an independent investigation conducted by Americans United for the Separation of Church and State discovered that chaplains at the Air Force Academy had repeatedly prodded evangelical cadets into proselytizing their nonevangelical classmates, who would otherwise, the chaplains said, "burn in the fires of hell." The academy's evangelical faculty members were cited for regularly introducing themselves to their classes as "born again" and encouraging their students to speak to them about their faith. A Christmas greeting, published in the academy's official newspaper and signed by three hundred members of the faculty and staff, including sixteen department heads and deputy heads as well as the dean of the faculty, not only declared that "Jesus Christ is the only real hope for the world" and that "there is salvation in no one else" but also encouraged cadets to seek out the signatories of the document in order to "discuss Jesus." The investigation concluded that these and other activities at the Air Force Academy constituted "egregious, systematic, and legally actionable violations of the Establishment Clause of the First Amendment to the United States Constitution."

Certainly, service members must be able to fulfill their spiritual needs (it should be noted that the Air Force Academy currently employs eighteen full-time chaplains and twenty-five reserve chaplains to attend to approximately four thousand cadets). But as the investigators who wrote the report for Americans United charged, the atmosphere of rampant evangelization at the Air Force Academy has become so pervasive that there is now a widespread perception among cadets that "to please their instructors, [they] should embrace the instructors' faith" and that "mimicking their superiors' religious beliefs and practices is necessary to succeed at the Academy."

It is obvious why these evangelical organizations have targeted the military. This is fertile ground for religious conversion, as Cadence International, a military missionary organization near Fort Jackson admits: "Deployment and possibly deadly combat are ever-present possibilities. [The cadets] are shaken. Shaken people are usually more ready to hear about God than those who are at ease, making them more responsive to the gospel."

However, there is something else at work here, as Cadence International itself admits. Military personnel are particularly valuable targets for conversion because, once converted, they have the ability to "spread the gospel as they move from assignment to assignment." The fact is, the systematic efforts of evangelical groups such as Cadence International, Christian Embassy, and Campus Crusade for Christ (to name but a handful of such organizations) to convert members of the military in a time of war is part of a larger, coordinated initiative to use American soldiers deployed in Iraq and Afghanistan—countries where Christian missionaries are not welcomed—to convert Muslims to evangelical Christianity. An investigation by the McClatchy Newspapers found that American soldiers dressed in military fatigues and surrounded by tanks and armored Humvees have been passing out New Testaments and evangelical pamphlets while out on patrol. "I am able to give [Iraqis] tracts on how to be saved, printed in Arabic," Captain Steve Mickel, an army chaplain in Iraq, enthused. "I wish I had enough Arabic Bibles to give them as well."

Some Iraqi children have received colorful comic books depicting Muslims burning in hell for not accepting Jesus as their savior. At a checkpoint in Fallujah, the scene of a gruesome U.S. offensive against Sunni insurgents in 2004, U.S. marines were caught handing out shiny coins to Iraqis crossing into the town. One side of the coin asked in Arabic, "Where will you spend eternity?" The other side had a verse from the Gospel of John: "For God so loved the world that He gave His only begotten Son, that whoever believes in Him shall not perish, but have eternal life."

"Because we are weak this is happening," said a shop owner in Fallujah when given one of these coins—the comment as much a threat as a statement of fact.

Such actions violate the U.S. military code of conduct, which expressly forbids soldiers from proselytizing their religion while serving in foreign countries, and more than a few service members have been severely reprimanded for doing so. Yet it may be difficult to fault these men and women in uniform for treating the wars in Afghanistan and Iraq as missionary opportunities when, from the start, both campaigns, and indeed the larger ideological conflict with Jihadism that the campaigns are supposed to represent, have been deliberately imbued with cosmic significance by their superiors. When the commander in chief of the armed forces declares that God instructed him to remove al-Qa'ida from Afghanistan and to strike at Saddam Hussein in Iraq, as the Israeli newspaper *Ha'aretz* reported Bush as saying in 2003; when the secretary of defense, Donald Rumsfeld, emblazons the president's top-secret briefings with what the journalist and Bush biographer Robert Draper calls "Crusades-like messaging" and verses from the Bible ("Therefore put on the full armor of God, so that when the day of evil comes, you may be able to stand your ground, and after you have done everything, to stand" Ephesians 6:11–13); when the secretary of the army, Pete Geren, explicitly defines the war in Iraq as a battle between America and "radical Islam" during a commencement speech at West Point; when the head of the U.S. military chaplains in Afghanistan, Lieutenant-Colonel Gary Hensley, exhorts his soldiers to "hunt down" the country's Muslim population for Jesus ("Get the hound of heaven after them," Hensley was caught on tape saying, "so we get them into the kindgom. That's what we do, that's our business"); when the largest and most powerful defense contractor in Iraq and Afghanistan, Blackwater, is headed by a man, Eric Prince, who, according to a former employee, views himself as "a Christian crusader tasked with eliminating Muslims and the Islamic faith from the globe," it is difficult to imagine how these young, pious, and "shaken" soldiers could construe their military mission, and indeed the entire War on Terror, in any way other than as part of a new crusade—a cosmic war—between the forces of good (us) and evil (them).

No doubt that is how the Jihadists understand the U.S. mission. Indeed, the United States' conduct in both Iraq and Afghanistan—the evangelizing soldiers, the humiliation of Muslim prisoners forced under torture to eat pork and curse Muhammad, the Crusader rhetoric of the military officers and political leaders—has not only validated the Jihadist argument that these wars are "a new Crusader campaign for the Islamic world" conducted by "the Devil's army," it has provided Jihadists with the opportunity to successfully present themselves as the last line of defense against the forces that seek to "annihilate Islam."

For bin Laden in particular, the war in Iraq has become a call to arms for Muslims everywhere to awake from their slumber, to embrace Islam's own tradition of cosmic war, and to take the battle directly to the enemies of God. "To my brother holy warriors in Iraq," he wrote at the height of the U.S. military campaign in that country, "to the heroes of Baghdad, the house of the caliphate—and all around; to the Ansar al-Islam, the descendants of Saladin; to the free men of Baquba, Mosul, and al-Anbar; to those who have emigrated for the sake of God to fight for the victory of their religion, leaving their fathers and sons, leaving their family and homeland . . . the Romans have gathered under the Banner of the Cross to fight the nation of beloved Muhammad. . . . Lord, give us patience, make us stand firm and help us struggle against the infidels. God [will be] victorious."

# CHAPTER FIVE

# The Near and the Far

The town of Tuz Khormato lies a little more than a hundred miles north of Baghdad, in Iraq's Salah ad-Din province. It is an ethnically and religiously mixed city of Sunnis, Shi'ites, Kurds, and Turkmen, which may explain why it has attracted so much attention from the mostly foreign Jihadists in the country who make up what the U.S. military calls al-Qa'ida in Iraq, or AQI (to differentiate the group from al-Qa'ida Central, Osama bin Laden's organization, which is based near the border of Pakistan and Afghanistan and seems to have little operational control over its Iraqi franchise). Since the American invasion in 2003, Tuz Khormato has been targeted by wave after wave of Jihadist militants who have journeyed to Iraq from countries as far away as the Philippines and Malaysia to wage war against those they call "infidels" and "hypocrites."

These two terms—infidel (*kafir*) and hypocrite (*munafiq*)—have become permanent fixtures in the Jihadist lexicon. Both words have quite specific meanings in the Qur'an. *Kafir* is the term most often used to designate the powerful pagan rulers of pre-Islamic Mecca, the

Quraysh, who fought a bloody, decadelong war with the nascent Muslim community. *Munafiq* is the term reserved for Arab tribes that joined the Muslim community, but only for political or material gain, and ultimately abandoned the new faith and returned to their old tribal ways. In Jihadism, however, both words have been stripped of their historical context, so that infidel has come to mean anyone who is not a Muslim, while hypocrite means any Muslim who is not a Jihadist. Both groups are designated as "unbelievers"; both are marked for death.

Jihadism is a puritanical movement in the sense that its members consider themselves to be the only true Muslims. All other Muslims are impostors or apostates who must repent of their "hypocrisy" or be abandoned to their fate. As an exclusively Sunni movement, Jihadism reserves particular contempt for the Shi'a (approximately 15 to 20 percent of the Muslim world and centered around Iran, Iraq, and the Levant), whom the Jihadists regard not as Muslims but as *rawafidah,* or "rejectionists"—heretics who are considered worse than the infidels and hypocrites. The Jordanian Jihadist Abu Musab al-Zarqawi, a petty thief and barely literate brute who was, until his death in 2006, the leader of al-Qa'ida in Iraq, argued that the Shi'a were a far graver threat to Islam than even the Americans. Shi'ism is "patent polytheism," Zarqawi claimed, a religion that "has nothing in common with Islam." The Shi'a are "the most evil of mankind . . . the lurking snake, the crafty and malicious scorpion, the spying enemy, the penetrating venom." Through random kidnappings, torture, and beheading of Shi'a civilians, Zarqawi almost single-handedly launched a sectarian civil war in Iraq.

Tuz Khormato, with its large Shi'ite population, became a favorite hunting ground for Zarqawi's roaming death squads. Jihadist suicide bombers linked to al-Qa'ida in Iraq have incinerated crowded restaurants and cafés. Tuz Khormato's market was practically razed by a car bomb. Improvised explosive devices have decimated the town's already anemic police force. In 2005, Tuz Khormato's main Shi'ite mosque was nearly burned to the ground. Mass graves have been unearthed on the outskirts of town, some of them filled with the bodies of women and children, their corpses bound, a few without heads.

Somehow, Tuz Khormato thrives. Despite the barbarity inflicted upon its people, the city has not undergone the same level of internal displacement and ethnic homogenization that one sees in Baghdad, where entire neighborhoods have been cleansed of any hint of diversity. The people of Tuz Khormato have known one another too long, have lived next to one another too long, have married and buried one another too long to be pried apart by a gang of militant puritans. And for that they have paid a price. The city bears the scars of their defiance. In the center of town, at the edge of what used to be a parking lot, is a crater the size of a Humvee.

It was the last day of Ramadan, Eid al-Fitr, a holiday like no other in Islam, when friends and families gather to exchange gifts and break the monthlong fast together. Little girls put on their new dresses, boys don spit-shined shoes, and, after twenty-eight long, hot days of denial and deprivation, everyone spills outdoors for a night of food and celebration.

The elders of Tuz Khormato had cleared out a parking lot for Eid and set up a makeshift carnival complete with swings and a slide, a rusty metal merry-go-round, and a small, hand-cranked Ferris wheel that creaked and groaned with each unsteady rotation. Confection booths sold sodas, snacks, and balloons. Lamps were lit. Music blared from loudspeakers.

The sun had just set when a young man walked onto the playground leading a horse-drawn cart filled with candy and toys. He was a stranger in Tuz Khormato; no one recognized him. But who knew anyone anymore? The war had fractured the country. Every day a new batch of refugees from Baghdad or Diyala or nearby Kirkuk arrived in Tuz Khormato—broken families, destitute widows, single men trying to remake their lives in a new town.

The young man stopped his cart in the center of the playground and began shouting out his wares. He opened the cart and pulled out a couple of chocolate bars, a stuffed animal, a small plastic soccer ball. Children jumped up from their games, abandoned the rides, rushed toward the cart, clasping wrinkled bills in their hands—money they had received from uncles and aunts and grandparents for making it through the difficult month. They waved the bills in the air, calling out their orders as they ran. But the young man was in no rush. He waited patiently for the girls in their new dresses and the boys in their new shoes to gather around him, to come close enough to touch, before calmly lifting the top of his candy cart, flipping a switch, and blowing himself up. A monstrous plume of black smoke hovered over the playground, blotting out the last light of the sun.

It is tempting, even comforting, to consider such abominable acts of terror to be the result of irrational or pathological behavior. But the truth is that terrorism is almost always a calculated choice. Terror is purposefully chosen, because it is often seen as the most effective, most expedient, and most economical method of pursuing a group's aims.

Still, there is something uniquely repulsive about the tactic of suicide terrorism, even more so when it is framed as a religious act. Suicide terrorism is by no means a distinctly Islamic or even religious phenomenon. The tactic was popularized by the Marxist militants of the Tamil Tigers during their violent insurgency against the Sri Lankan government. Robert Pape, a political scientist at the University of Chicago, has compiled a database of every suicide attack that took place in every part of the world from 1980 to 2003. His data demonstrate that "there is little connection between suicide terrorism and Islamic fundamentalism, or any one of the world's religions." In Pape's database, secular groups account for a third of all suicide attacks. There is, it seems, a simple reason why suicide has become such a common method of terrorism: it works. When one's adversary possesses the most formidable military hardware, when its strength cannot be challenged in battle, suicide terrorism levels the playing field. As a Palestinian militant coldly explained to an Israeli reporter, "We have no planes or missiles, not even artillery with which to fight evil. The most effective instrument for inflicting harm with a minimum of losses is this type of [suicide] mission." Put crudely, the suicide terrorist has become the poor man's smart bomb.

Nevertheless, there is no question that killing and dying are always easier to justify if they can be framed as ritual or ceremonial acts, which is why Jihadists refer to suicide terrorism as "martyrdom operations." This is not a euphemism but an earnest attempt to infuse death with a sense of cosmic significance. It seems not to matter that, on the topic of suicide, the Qur'an is absolutely clear: "Do not kill yourself; if someone does so [God] shall cast him into Hell" (4:29–30). Nor does it seem important that countless sayings (Hadith) of the Prophet Muhammad refer to the gruesome punishment that awaits those who take their own lives: "Whoever purposely throws himself from a mountain and kills himself, he will forever be falling into the fire of Hell, wherein he will abide eternally; whoever drinks poison and kills himself with it, he will forever be carrying his poison in his hand and drinking it in the fire of Hell, wherein he will abide eternally; whoever kills himself with an iron weapon, will forever be carrying that weapon in his hand and stabbing his abdomen with it in the fire of Hell, wherein he will abide eternally." The Qur'an is equally unambiguous in its injunction against killing women, children, the elderly, protected minorities, and, most significantly, other Muslims. Some Jihadist ideologues go to great lengths to try to justify both suicide terrorism and attacks against fellow Muslims or civilian targets ("If the unbelievers kill young and old," argues Yusuf al-Ayiri, the Saudi Jihadist who was once bin Laden's bodyguard, "then Muslims should be permitted to do the same"). Yet even bin Laden has stated that "the one issue on which all people are agreed, even if they themselves have been the victims of oppression and hostility, is that you cannot kill innocent children."

The truth is, there is no religious argument in Islam for the crime of murdering Muslim children at play. And so, for the most part, Jihadists do not bother making one. Instead, they put forth a simple proposition: The universe is divided into two. On one side are "the people of heaven"; on the other, "the people of hell." There is no middle ground. If you are not on one side, then you are on the other. If you are not *us*, then you are *them*. If you are them, then it does not matter whether you are a soldier or not, a child or not, a Muslim or not. In a cosmic war one is either with God or against God. No one is innocent. In the words of a member of Algeria's Armed Islamic Group (GIA), "There is no neutrality in the war we are waging. With the exception of those who are with us, all others are apostates and deserve to die."

There is a term in Islam for this uncompromising moral dichotomy: *al-wala' wal-bara'*. It is difficult to render this phrase into English. *Al-wala' wal-bara'* can mean "loyalty and enmity," "allegiance and disavowal," or even "love and hate." According to the al-Qa'ida ideologue Muhammad Saeed al-Qahtani, *"Wala'* inspires intimacy, concern and help. *Bara'* provokes obstruction, enmity and rejection."

However the phrase is translated, *al-wala' wal-bara'* suggests a *cosmic duality*, in which the whole of creation is partitioned into "believers"—by which Jihadists mean themselves—and "unbelievers"—a category that includes non-Muslims; Shi'ite Muslims; Muslims living in Europe or America, which Jihadists refer to as *dar al-kufr* ("the land of unbelief"); the rulers and governments of the Arab and Muslim world; the clerical leaders of Islam's traditional religious institutions and schools of law ("imams of infidelity," Jihadists call them); and anyone who accepts such political or religious authority. "The difference between the unbelievers and believers," Maulana Masood Azhar, founder of Jaish-e Mohammed, writes in his book *Virtues of the Jihad*, "is similar to the difference between light and darkness."

Although long a fringe doctrine in Islamic thought, one not found in the Qur'an and totally abandoned by contemporary Islamic scholars, *al-wala' wal-bara'* has, in Jihadism, become "the very foundation of the religion," to quote Zarqawi's spiritual mentor, the Palestinian Jihadist Abu Muhammad al-Maqdisi. The aforementioned Al-Qahtani considers the doctrine to be inherent in the Muslim declaration of faith: "There is no god but God." The *shahadah*, as this statement is called, is, for the Jihadist, both an affirmation and a denial. It is simultaneously an acceptance of God's law and a rejection of the laws of the world. In the minds of the Jihadists, the *shahadah* demands not only the promotion of virtue but also the proscription of vice; not only love of God but hatred of God's enemies. "If you were sincere," writes Abu Hamza al-Masri, the one-eyed Jihadist preacher who briefly led the Finsbury Park Mosque in North London, "if you really loved God, you'd hate even the shadow of [the unbeliever]." Ayman Zawahiri puts it more simply: "Whoever loves an infidel is an infidel."

The power of *al-wala' wal-bara'* as a religious doctrine derives from its ability to unilaterally proclaim someone an infidel, or *kafir*—a practice known in Jihadist circles as *takfir*. Islam has no means of excommunicating a Muslim. There is not, nor has there ever been, a centralized religious authority with the power to declare who is and who is not a Muslim. The practice of *takfir*, however, places that authority into the hands of individual believers, allowing them to simply declare their Muslim enemies to be "unbelievers," thereby avoiding any religious prohibitions against shedding Muslim blood. Jihadists use *takfir* with remarkable skill, applying it to those who disagree with any aspect of their worldview, for example Muslims who vote or take part in the political process: "Those who believe in democracy and they vote and they don't mind being elected or to make laws when they have a chance. These people are *kuffar* [plural of *kafir*]," writes al-Masri in his book *Beware of Takfir*. "It does not matter how much worship they do or how many times they go on Hajj [pilgrimage], they cannot come an inch closer to Islam because of this action."

Over the centuries, numerous fatwas, or religious declarations, have been issued by Muslim clerics denouncing the practice of *takfir* as a usurpation of God's judgment (the practice has no basis in the Qur'an). In 2005, one hundred seventy of the world's leading clerics and religious scholars, representing every sect, schism, and school of law in Islam, gathered in Amman, Jordan, to issue a joint fatwa "to reaffirm that there is no [such thing as] *takfir*" and that no Muslim is allowed to label any other Muslim an apostate for any reason. The response from the Jihadists was to proclaim everyone who took part in the Amman conference an apostate deserving of death. Almost four months to the day in which the declaration against *takfir* was issued, four suicide terrorists, sent from Iraq by Zarqawi, blew themselves up in a series of coordinated attacks in Amman, killing sixty people, most of them Muslims.

Practitioners of *takfir* usually justify the doctrine by referencing the writings of one of Islam's most revered legal theorists, Ahmad ibn Taymiyyah. Born in 1263 C.E., ibn Taymiyyah is widely acknowledged to be one of the greatest thinkers in Islamic history, a philosopher and theologian whose immense oeuvre—he wrote more than three hundred individual works—and famed piety led his disciples to give him the title of Shaykh al-Islam, an honor reserved only for the most supreme legal authorities.

Ibn Taymiyyah was reared in a family of prominent religious scholars. Both his father and his grandfather belonged to the Hanbali School of Law, the most conservative of the four schools in Sunni Islam (the other three are the Hanafi, the Maliki, and the Shafi'i). A diligent student who had memorized the Qur'an before he was nine years old, ibn Taymiyyah joined his father and grandfather as a Hanbali cleric at the astonishingly young age of nineteen—though, significantly, only after he had spent a number of years under the tutelage of major scholars from the other three schools of law, an unusual practice at the time, especially for someone from such an ultraconservative background. The decision to dabble so deeply in other schools may have annoyed his father and grandfather, but the experience provided ibn Taymiyyah with a comparative perspective on legal issues that would, in later years, allow him to challenge certain Hanbali orthodoxies in a way that had rarely been attempted.

Ibn Taymiyyah's family hailed from the ancient city of Haran, near Baghdad, the seat of the Abbasid Empire and the cultural and political capital of the Muslim world. Situated at the crossroads of half a dozen different trade routes and nourished by the life-giving waters of the

Tigris and the Euphrates, Baghdad (the name means "the gift of God," in Persian) was the wealthiest and, with approximately one million inhabitants, most populous city in the world. It was also the most learned; it is said that every citizen in Baghdad was expected to know how to read and write. While Europe was mired in the Dark Ages, a steady stream of scholars and artisans from every corner of the world, of every religion and ethnicity, flowed into Baghdad to study medicine, mathematics, astronomy, and the arts. A corps of royal scribes worked day and night translating the accumulated knowledge of the Western world from Greek, Latin, Syriac, Sanskrit, and Persian into Arabic, the lingua franca of the arts and sciences. The texts were transferred from ancient scraps of parchment and papyrus onto fresh sheets of paper, made in Baghdad's very own paper mill (the first paper mill in the world), and placed inside the legendary Library of Baghdad—known in Arabic as *bayt al-hakma* or "the House of Wisdom"—where they were preserved for future generations. (Were it not for the work of these scribes, the world might well have lost track of Plato, Aristotle, Pythagoras, Euclid, Plotinus, and the rest of the foundation of Western philosophy, much of which was translated into European languages from Arabic.) Algebra was invented in the Library of Baghdad; so was the science of optics. Anatomy and physiology, music and meteorology, logic and philosophy, all were developed or advanced by the scholars who made Baghdad their home.

Alas, such a glorious city—such magnificent bathhouses and terraced gardens, such fountains, mosques, museums, and libraries—could not escape the notice of the Mongol warrior who would come to be known as "the devourer of cities." At the dawn of the thirteenth century, Genghis Khan united the nomadic tribes scattered along the grass-fed steppes of the Central Asian plateau into a mobile machine of death and destruction. In just a few years, Genghis's army had swept through modern-day China, Russia, Afghanistan, and India, razing entire towns and slaughtering millions of people (eighteen million, by some estimates). The Mongol horsemen continued westward, descending upon the legendary cities of Iran—Merv, Nishapur, Samarkand—

laying waste to everything, killing everyone in sight, uprooting graves, flattening buildings, looting, pillaging, burning.

In 1258, the Mongol army, led by Genghis's grandson Hülegü Khan, arrived at the gates of Baghdad. As per Mongol custom, Hülegü sent an emissary to the Abbasid caliph, al-Mustasim, giving him the option of laying down his arms and surrendering the city. When the caliph refused, Hülegü's army forced its way through Baghdad's fortified walls and unleashed a brutal punishment upon its inhabitants.

The Mongols burned everything. The books in the Library of Baghdad were flung into the Tigris, turning the waters black with ink. Al-Mustasim's family was massacred, down to the last child. The caliph himself was wrapped in a rug and kicked to death. No one was spared. Hülegü's army rounded up Baghdad's scholars, scribes, and artisans and chopped off their heads. The bodies they left to be picked clean by the birds. The heads they piled into a giant pyramid in the center of the city. The stench of decay carried for miles. By the time the Mongols' thirst for blood had been sated, Baghdad had been practically depopulated.

Somehow, in the midst of the devastation, ibn Taymiyyah's family managed to flee to Damascus, leaving behind everything but their books. Yet they could not escape the Mongol horde. Four years after the fall of Baghdad, in 1260 C.E., the Mongols entered Syria and sacked Damascus. Three years later, in 1263 C.E., Ahmad ibn Taymiyyah was born.

The profound social upheaval that followed the Mongol invasion left its mark on ibn Taymiyyah. He came of age at a time of religious uncertainty, compounded by the fact that the descendents of Hülegü, rather than moving on to other conquests, had begun to settle in the occupied Muslim lands and even to adopt Islam as their religion. The Mongols were actually quite tolerant of other faiths, and they easily absorbed Islamic beliefs and practices into their own shamanistic spiritual system, creating a kind of hybrid of Sunni Islam and Eastern paganism. This created a dilemma for Muslims under Mongol rule, many of whom did not know how to respond to the conversion of their new and unfamiliar masters. Now that the Mongols had become Muslims, must they be obeyed as God's regents on earth? Should the same people who only a few years before had killed millions of Muslims, enslaved their children, plundered their property, burned their mosques, and uprooted their graves now be considered Muslims just because they had declared that "there is no god but God"?

It was ibn Taymiyyah's simple yet revolutionary answer to these questions, written in the form of a fatwa (an official religious ruling), that set him apart from his fellow Hanbali scholars and made him the hero of Jihadism that he is today. The Mongols, ibn Taymiyyah wrote, are "unbelievers [and] hypocrites who do not really believe in Islam . . . every type of hypocrisy, unbelief, and outright rejection of the faith is found among the Mongol followers. They are among the most ignorant of all people, who least know the faith and are far from following it." They were, in short, apostates and need not be obeyed.

What made this fatwa extraordinary was that it violated the most basic tenet of Hanbali doctrine, established by the founder of the Hanbali school, Ahmad ibn Hanbal (780–855 C.E.), which stated that the leader of the Islamic state, whether a caliph, a sultan, or an imam, had been placed in his exalted position by God and thus had to be obeyed regardless of his actions or his piety. "Jihad is valid with the imams, whether they act justly or evilly," ibn Hanbal declared. "The Friday worship, the two Feasts, and the Pilgrimage (are observed) with [the sultans], even if they are not upright, just, and pious. Taxes are paid to [the caliphs], whether they deal justly or wickedly." For ibn Hanbal, social order had to be maintained at all costs. No matter how "un-Islamic" the actions of a Muslim leader may appear, his rule must be followed.

Ibn Taymiyyah disagreed with his master. To live freely and justly as Muslims required a leader committed to Islamic guidance, he argued. If that leader failed in his duty to uphold Muslim principles and did not abide by Islamic law, then he was not really a Muslim but a *kafir;* his rule was invalid. Ibn Taymiyyah declared that it was incumbent upon all Muslims under the rule of an impious leader to rebel. Employing the practice of *takfir,* he even went so far as to argue that any Muslim who was willing to abide by the rule of the *kafir* leader was himself a *kafir.*

There was precedent for such an extremist view. Six hundred years earlier, a sect called the Kharijites had made a similar argument when they rebelled against the leadership of the third caliph, Uthman ibn Affan. The Kharijites believed that the leader of the Muslim community must be blameless and without sin. He must exceed all other Muslims in his piety and learning; otherwise he had no right to lead the community and must be removed from power by any means necessary.

Ibn Taymiyyah was certainly no Kharijite, but he agreed that it was the obligation of every Muslim to ensure the purity of the community by purging it of all innovation (*bida'*) and heresy. He also drew inspiration from the Kharijites in proposing a strict geographical division of the world into realms of belief (*dar al-Islam*) and unbelief (*dar al-kufr*), with the former in constant pursuit of the latter. But although he lived on the Anatolian frontier, where Christian and Muslim forces continued to clash with one another long after the Crusades had ceased, ibn Taymiyyah focused his attention strictly on the enemy living inside *dar al-Islam*—that is, on his fellow Muslims who did not adequately follow Islamic law; on those he considered "heretics," such as the Shi'a, whom ibn Taymiyyah despised; and most especially on the Mongol invaders, who despite claiming to be Muslims were, in ibn Taymiyyah's view, apostates against whom it was incumbent upon all Muslims to declare jihad. "To fight the Mongols who came to Syria," he wrote, "is a duty prescribed [to all]."

Ibn Taymiyyah reconceptualized jihad as an "individual obligation" (*fard 'ala l'ayn*), overturning centuries of consensus among his fellow legal scholars that jihad must be a "collective obligation" (*fard 'ala l-kifaya*)—a defensive struggle against oppression and injustice that could be authorized only by a qualified imam. Jihad, for ibn Taymiyyah, was an *offensive* weapon that could be employed, on one's own and without guidance, to propagate Islam, to purify it and make it prevail over the whole of the globe. Indeed, Ibn Taymiyyah elevated jihad into the highest form of devotion. "Jihad implies all kinds of worship," he wrote in *The Religious and Moral Doctrine of Jihad.* "It is the best voluntary act that man can perform . . . it is better than the hajj (greater pilgrimage) and the 'umrah (lesser pilgrimage), better than voluntary salaat (prayer) and voluntary fasting."

Ibn Taymiyyah spent many years in prison for his writings and ultimately died there in 1328 C.E. Although his disciples, and in particular his secretary and successor, ibn Qayyim al-Jawziyyah, managed to keep his teachings alive for a generation or two, copying his works and sharing them with others, for most scholars, ibn Taymiyyah's opinions regarding what he called "apostate rulers" were deemed dangerous and far too radical. By the end of the fourteenth century, when the Ottomans began reclaiming Muslim lands from Mongol rule, the great Shaykh al-Islam had been more or less forgotten, until six hundred years later, in the tumultuous political landscape of postcolonial Egypt, when ibn Taymiyyah's stark division of the world into spheres of belief and unbelief, his bold use of *takfir* against the Muslim rulers of his day, and his elevation of jihad into a form of devotion was dramatically resurrected by a group of radical Islamists in an attempt to overthrow the Egyptian government and launch a revolution across the Arab world.

October 6, 1981. As Egypt's president, Anwar al-Sadat, Gamal Abd al-Nasser's handpicked successor, stood on a platform watching a military parade march before him in commemoration of Egypt's war with Israel in 1973, a lieutenant in the Egyptian army named Khalid Islambouli, along with three other men, suddenly broke formation and rushed toward the presidential platform, lobbing grenades and firing wildly. "Death to the pharaoh!" Islambouli was heard shouting as he emptied his rifle into Sadat's chest.

Khalid Islambouli was a member of the Egyptian Islamic Jihad (EIJ), one of dozens of Jihadist organizations centered in and around Cairo University, a place brimming with radical activists of every stripe. Most of these groups had little in common, save for their hatred of the government and their sense of betrayal by the Muslim Brotherhood, which had become increasingly accommodating in its interactions with Egypt's political establishment. The members of the various organizations were mostly young, middle-class professionals—scientists, engineers, schoolteachers, bureaucrats—the best and brightest of Egyptian society. But they were also profoundly dissatisfied with the spiritual decline of Egyptian society and were prepared to lash out against those whom they felt were sullying the purity of the Muslim community. One group in particular, Takfir wal-Hijra, led by two shadowy Jihadist figures known as Sayyid Imam (aka Dr. Fadl) and Shukri Mustafa, had so fully absorbed the practice of *takfir* that they began kidnapping and executing members of the religious establishment whom they deemed to be apostates.

In the wake of Anwar al-Sadat's assassination, more than three hundred members of these radical organizations were rounded up and thrown into prison. At their trial, prosecutors presented an unusual document, written by one of Islambouli's coconspirators, Muhammad Abd al-Salam Faraj, entitled "The Neglected Duty." This brief and somewhat convoluted pamphlet had never been intended for public consumption. It was, rather, an internal document brimming with a jumble of legal and theological arguments meant to justify Sadat's murder and answer the objections that were bound to arise from Egypt's clerical class, particularly the scholars of al-Azhar, that this was a legitimate act.

Faraj based his justification for the assassination squarely on the writings of ibn Taymiyyah. "The rulers of this age are in apostasy from Islam," he wrote, channeling the famed Hanbali jurist. "They carry nothing from Islam but their names, even though they pray and fast and claim to be Muslim." According to Faraj, even Mongol rule would be better than "the laws which the West has imposed on countries like Egypt and which have no connection with Islam or with any other revealed religion." Faraj argued that by signing a peace treaty with Israel (the 1978 Camp David Accords) at the urging of U.S. President Jimmy

Carter, Sadat had committed a grave sin. He had forfeited the right to be called a Muslim. He was a *kafir;* it was now the duty of every Muslim to shed his blood.

"The Neglected Duty" laid out, for the first time, the aspirations of the nascent Jihadist movement. Chief among these was the reestablishment of the Caliphate, which had been abolished after World War I by the founder of the modern secular state of Turkey, Mustafa Kemal Atatürk. For a great many Muslims, the destruction of the Caliphate had permanently fractured the worldwide community of faith, the *ummah,* which the Prophet Muhammad had established fourteen centuries before, into competing nation-states. As Sayyid Qutb, perhaps the most influential of all Jihadist ideologues, claimed, with the end of the Caliphate, the Muslim community had essentially reverted to a state of *jahaliyyah*—the time of ignorance and idolatry that existed before the introduction to Islam.

"If we look at the sources and foundations of modern ways of living, it becomes clear that the whole world is steeped in *jahaliyyah,*" Qutb wrote in his celebrated manifesto *Milestones.* "This *jahaliyyah* is based on rebellion against God's sovereignty on earth. It transfers to man one of the greatest attributes of God, namely sovereignty, and makes some men lords over others. . . . [It claims] the right to create values, to legislate rules of collective behavior, and to choose any way of life that rests with men, without regard to what God Almighty has prescribed." In other words, for Qutb, as for many in the Jihadist movement, the end of the Caliphate had signaled the end of the *ummah.*

Faraj, however, was adamant that the Caliphate could not be built "without the support of an Islamic state." Jihadism, at the time, was still very much an Islamist movement, focused not on global transformation but on overthrowing local governments. "To fight an enemy who is near," Faraj wrote, "is more important than to fight an enemy who is far."

Not surprisingly, the response from the esteemed scholars at al-Azhar to Faraj's justification for Sadat's murder was swift and dismissive. The arguments presented in "The Neglected Duty" were rebutted by no less than the grand mufti of Egypt, Sheikh Jadd al-Haqq, the country's highest religious authority, whose point-by-point refutation of Faraj's polemic was published in *Al-Ahram*, the country's largest newspaper, for all to read. Written in the form of a fatwa (to emphasize his legal authority over Faraj, who was not a cleric), al-Haqq branded the Jihadists as "Kharijites" and took direct aim at Faraj's contention that Egypt could not be considered an Islamic country, that its political and religious rulers were apostates. "The prayer ceremonies are executed, mosques are opened everywhere, religious taxes are paid, people make the pilgrimage to Mecca, and the rule of Islam is widespread," al-Haqq argued. Perhaps there were certain matters, such as the practice of usury, in which the government did not fully abide by Islamic law, but, according to al-Haqq, "this does not make the country, the people, the rulers, and the ruled apostates."

Of course, the grand mufti had altogether missed the point of "The Neglected Duty." Faraj was not recommending how Egypt could become more Islamic in its laws and practices, and he certainly was not interested in engaging in a theological argument with someone whose religious authority he did not accept as valid. Nor was he proposing an alternative standard of governance that would be more suitable to him and his Jihadist colleagues; nothing of the sort exists in "The Neglected Duty." Lost in the debates and discussions that took place among the scholars of al-Azhar over the validity of Faraj's views was the fact that neither he nor any of the assassins had made any preparations whatsoever for what was to be done after Sadat's death. It appeared that the thought had never even crossed their minds. Such human preparations seemed unnecessary, as Faraj's translator Johannes Jansen notes, since the Jihadists assumed that "God himself will take care of everything once the Muslims have taken the initiative to obey his command to *jihad* and have opened fire on the unbelievers." When Faraj was questioned about his plans for establishing an Islamic state as the first step toward reestablishing the Caliphate, he replied, "The establishment of an Islamic state is the execution of a divine command. We are not responsible for its results . . . when the rule of the infidel has fallen, everything will be in the hands of the Muslims." What use were human preparations when one was battling a cosmic war against "the armies of the pharaoh," as he called the Egyptian military—a war that transcends the bounds of history?

Faraj was executed, along with Islambouli and two other members of Egyptian Islamic Jihad, for his role in Sadat's assassination. The rest of the Jihadists rounded up by the Egyptian police served various years in prison before being released. Among those arrested was a bookish, bespectacled surgeon from Maadi, a wealthy suburb of Cairo, named Ayman Zawahiri.

Born to a successful, affluent family of scholars and physicians, Zawahiri had joined the Egyptian Muslim Brotherhood as a young man but, like Islambouli and Faraj, had left the group when it decided to abandon violence in favor of social engagement. After the execution of Sayyid Qutb, whom he greatly admired, Zawahiri gathered together a few of his university friends into a small underground cell committed to overthrowing Nasser's regime and replacing it with an Islamic state. His was an amateurish operation, but after Nasser had died and been replaced with Anwar Sadat, Zawahiri managed to merge his organization with a few others to form Egyptian Islamic Jihad, or EIJ.

Though he would later boast of being one of EIJ's leading organizers, Zawahiri claimed not to have been aware of the plot against Sadat until the morning of the assassination. He confessed to the Egyptian police that he had been "astonished and shaken," when told of Islambouli's plan and wanted nothing to do with it. Regardless, Zawahiri was thrown into jail, where, under torture, he betrayed his allies and fellow EIJ members to the Egyptian authorities. Since it was determined that he had played no direct role in the plot against Sadat, he was released after serving only five years and promptly fled Egypt for the city of Peshawar on the border of Pakistan and Afghanistan, where he took a position with the Red Crescent, treating Arab soldiers wounded in the war against the Soviets (the Soviet Union had invaded Afghanistan in 1979).

Afghanistan in the 1980s had become a safe haven for Jihadists fleeing persecution in their home countries, just as, two decades earlier, Saudi Arabia had become a haven for the Salafists and radical members of the Muslim Brotherhood. The Jihadists viewed the Afghan war as a training ground to learn vital combat and guerrilla skills that would assist them in their nationalist struggles back home. Dozens of independent Jihadist groups from Tunisia, Egypt, Turkey, Algeria, and Turkmenistan had established bases throughout the area. Almost all these groups were still narrowly focused on the Near Enemy and had not yet shifted their consciousness onto the global plane. Though they may have been united against the Soviet invasion, they had very little else in common. Each camp followed its own leader, and each represented a different current, school, doctrine, or ideology within the larger Jihadist movement. There were the Uzbek Mujahidin, the Islamic Fighting Group in Morocco, the Libyan Islamic Fighting Group, Dr. Fadl's Takfir wal-Hijra, Zawahiri's Egyptian Islamic Jihad (which he had reconstituted under his leadership in order to plot the overthrow of Hosni Mubarak, Sadat's successor, the new pharaoh), another Jihadist group from Egypt called the Egyptian Islamic Group, the Ghuraba (the camp of the Syrian Jihadist Abu Musab al-Suri), and a camp called Maktab al-Khadamat al-Mujahidin al-Arab ("Office of the Services to the Arab Mujahidin"), or MAK, which was headed by a charismatic Palestinian activist named Abdullah Yusuf Azzam and his shy, lanky protégé and chief financier, Osama bin Laden.

Bin Laden had met Azzam, a former Muslim Brotherhood activist who had fled from Jordan to Saudi Arabia in 1973, at the prestigious King Abdul Aziz University, where the young Saudi was enrolled as a student of engineering. Though employed as a professor of Islamic jurisprudence at the university, Azzam focused the bulk of his attention on running the MAK, an international network funded by the Saudi government, whose purpose was to send fighters from all over the Muslim world to Afghanistan to battle the Soviet army. It was Azzam who, more than anyone else, helped popularize the burgeoning Jihadist movement. His widely read periodical, *Al-Jihad*, published in 1984, spread the ideology of global jihad to every corner of the Muslim world. By providing a snapshot of world events (especially the war in Afghanistan) as seen through the lens of Jihadism, Azzam almost single-handedly shifted the consciousness of local Jihadist groups to more global concerns. "Jihad is an obligation upon the whole earth from East to West," Azzam wrote in his book *Defense of the Muslim Lands*.

Abdullah Azzam made a deep and lasting impression on bin Laden. Born in Riyadh, the capital of Saudi Arabia, to a fabulously wealthy family with close ties to the royal family (his father, Muhammed bin Laden, owned a construction company that made him one of the richest "nonroyals" in the kingdom, Bin Laden, like so many of his fellow Saudis, had had very little knowledge of the world beyond the Arabian Peninsula. Azzam broadened bin Laden's world, giving him a global perspective on the struggle of Muslims in Afghanistan, Palestine, Chechnya, and Kashmir to gain independence and freedom from foreign oppression. So struck was he by the Palestinian revolutionary's zeal that three years after meeting him, in 1979, bin Laden completely abandoned his studies, dropped out of university, and moved with Azzam to Peshawar, where he helped his former teacher set up a series of guesthouses for the volunteer fighters who had, at Azzam's urging, begun pouring into the region to join the jihad against the Soviets.

It is not known when or under what circumstances Osama bin Laden first met Ayman Zawahiri. There were many camp leaders in Pakistan and Afghanistan vying for the wealthy Saudi's attention. What is clear is that his sojourn in the refugee camps on the Afghan border had radicalized Zawahiri even further, pushing him toward an acceptance of the doctrine of *takfir*, most eagerly advanced by his fellow Egyptian Dr. Fadl. The *takfir* ideology had been slowly spreading through the Jihadist camps like a virus, binding the various organizations together under a single collective identity and allowing them to divide the whole of the world into camps of belief (them) and unbelief (everyone else). *Takfir* became a tool to distinguish the Jihadist fighters from those they had left behind in their home countries: if you did not support the jihad in Afghanistan, you were a *kafir*; if you cooperated with Arab governments, you were a *kafir;* if you took religious advice from the clerical institutions, you were a *kafir.*

It was the doctrine of *takfir,* and Zawahiri's increasingly uncompromising acceptance of it, that would ultimately drive a wedge between him and Abdullah Azzam. Azzam was unconvinced about the usefulness of attacking fellow Muslims, even so-called heretic leaders. After all, he received a good deal of the money for his venture in Afghanistan from the Saudi state and had no interest in antagonizing the royals. An angry rivalry erupted between Azzam and Zawahiri for bin Laden's loyalty and, more important, his money. Zawahiri was desperate for bin Laden's financial support to fund his army of Egyptian Jihadists training for revolution in Egypt, while Azzam needed bin Laden to help him unite all the Jihadist camps in Afghanistan, irrespective of their national origins, into a global fighting force that could spread the jihad into Pakistan, Kashmir, and perhaps even Azzam's national home, Palestine.

In November 1989, just a few months after the last of the Soviet troops had withdrawn from Afghanistan in defeat, Abdullah Azzam was assassinated. To this day, no one knows who was responsible for his death, though the blame has long been placed on Zawahiri, who clearly wanted bin Laden's attention to himself. Yet even after Azzam's death, deep divisions remained between Zawahiri, who was still focused on the Near Enemy in Egypt, and bin Laden, who insisted on putting a stop to the internal divisions among the Jihadists by uniting all of the camps in Afghanistan under a single banner focused on the Far Enemy. According to Montasser al-Zayyat, Zawahiri's biographer, bin Laden "advised Zawahiri to stop armed operations in Egypt [altogether] and to ally with him against the common enemies: The United States and Israel."

At first, few Jihadists in Afghanistan, Zawahiri among them, accepted bin Laden's global focus. However, Iraq's invasion of Kuwait in 1990 and the Saudi regime's decision to invite U.S. forces into the kingdom to repel the Iraqi forces solidified bin Laden's case that the leaders of the Arab and Muslim world were mere puppets of the great superpowers and that the Jihadists should therefore focus their energies on the country pulling the strings, the United States. In any case, the money was with the Saudi, so Zawahiri and his fellow Jihadists had little choice but to fold their operations into bin Laden's (now loosely dubbed al-Qaʻida). The merging of Zawahiri's radical Salafism and bin Laden's Saudi Wahhabism to form a new, *global* version of Jihadism— one focused on the Far Enemy instead of the Near Enemy—would be formalized in 1998, when the two men, along with a handful of other Jihadist leaders, announced the creation of the World Islamic Front. The organization issued an official fatwa clarifying its new agenda: "To kill the Americans and their allies—*civilians and military*—is an individual duty (*fard ʻala lʻayn*) incumbent upon every Muslim" (emphasis added).

Jihadism, it seemed, had gone global. The rest, as they say, is history.

In the years since the creation of the World Islamic Front, in the aftermath of the attacks of 9/11 and the launch of the War on Terror, throughout the subsequent wars in Afghanistan and Iraq, Americans have repeatedly asked the same question: "Why do they hate us?" An entire cottage industry has arisen to answer this question.

There may have been numerous grievances that inspired the attacks, but the strategic *purpose* behind 9/11 is quite clear: "to awaken the Islamic Nation, which has been drugged, put to sleep and been absent from the confrontation . . . by imposing a confrontation between us and our real enemy [the West]," in the words of Abu Musab al-Suri. Al-Suri's assertion reinforces a fundamental truth about terrorism. These are not so much actions in pursuit of specific ends as they are symbolic statements of power directed at a carefully selected audience. Whatever political, economic, or military agenda may lie behind the act of terror is often secondary, and sometimes even irrelevant, to the more elemental aim of terrorism, which is, quite simply, to *terrorize*. (The word "terrorism" is derived from the Latin *terrere*, which means "to make someone tremble.") That is why the most potent weapon a terrorist has is neither a gun nor a bomb but a television camera. As a spectacular, even theatrical display of public violence, terrorism must have a captive audience; otherwise it is not terrorism.

The truth is that for the Jihadists who attacked the United States on 9/11, no goal was achieved, nor, perhaps, was any intended. The mere symbolism of bringing down the impregnable emblems of America's financial dominance and global military hegemony—with only a few box cutters and a will fortified by the divine—was itself the goal. Their ambition was not just to maim and kill but "to show the world how awesome was the form of power they—and they alone—possessed." Like the Zealots of ancient Palestine and the radical Religious Zionists of modern-day Israel, like the cross-marked knights of the Christian Crusades and the military missionaries in America's armed forces, these Jihadist militants are engaged in a ritual drama being waged on a cosmic plane. They cannot be negotiated with because they want nothing—at least, nothing that this world can offer them. Indeed, it is their utter lack of interest in achieving any kind of earthly victory that makes them such a distinctive and appealing force in the Muslim world. As the scholar of religions Bruce Lawrence writes, theirs is "a creed of great purity and intensity capable of inspiring [their] followers with a degree of passion and principled conviction that no secular movement in the Arab world has ever matched."

These Muslim cosmic warriors legitimize their attacks against both military and civilian targets, against both Muslims and non-Muslims, by dividing the world into what bin Laden calls "two separate camps, one of faith . . . and one of infidelity": *al-wala' wal-bara'*. They rely on the doctrine of *takfir* to justify the slaughter of women and children, the elderly and the ill. Although they are mostly holed up with the remnants of the Taliban in the tribal regions of the North-West Frontier Province on the border between Pakistan and Afghanistan, unlike the Taliban, they have no nationalist ambitions. Their jihad is not a defensive struggle against an occupying power but an eternal cosmic war that transcends all earthly ambitions. As Zawahiri declared, "Jihad in the path of God is greater than any individual or organization. It is a struggle between Truth and Falsehood, until God Almighty inherits the earth and those who live in it. [Taliban commander] Mullah Muhammad Omar and Sheikh Osama bin Laden—may Allah protect them from all evil—are merely two soldiers of Islam in the journey of Jihad, while the struggle between Truth and Falsehood transcends time."

To its credit, the U.S. military has had a fair measure of success rooting out and killing al-Qaʿida's cosmic warriors. In fact, as an international criminal conspiracy, al-Qaʿida faces nothing short of an existential crisis. Its infrastructure has been destroyed, its rank and file almost totally decimated. Although al-Qaʿida may maintain some level of operational control over a few of the Jihadist attacks that have taken place around the globe, and while it has proven it can still perpetrate horrific acts of violence, it no longer possesses the resources it enjoyed before 9/11. Its achievements since then have been chimerical at best. Not a single country has fallen into its hands. Iraq's Sunni insurgents, once allies of al-Qaʿida, have turned their backs on the organization because of its complete disregard for Islam's rules of war. The possibility of a reconstituted global Caliphate under the group's command is at this point too laughable to be taken seriously. It has in no way inspired the global Muslim uprising it intended when it changed its focus from the Near Enemy to the Far Enemy. On the contrary, poll after poll across the Muslim world has revealed overwhelming majorities among all classes, ages, and sectors of society condemning al-Qaʿida's actions. "Excuse me Mr. Zawahiri," read a recent post on a popular Jihadist website, "but who is it who is killing with Your Excellency's blessing, the innocents in Baghdad, Morocco and Algeria?"

Indeed, al-Qaʿida's wanton slaughter of innocent civilians and its liberal use of *takfir* to condemn to death anyone who disagrees with the group has turned even fellow Jihadists against it. In 2008, Dr. Fadl, the former head of Takfir wal-Hijra and the man most responsible for the spread of the doctrine of *takfir* among the Jihadist camps in Afghanistan, published a book denouncing al-Qaʿida and its leaders. "Zawahiri and bin Laden [are] extremely immoral," he told a reporter with the Saudi daily *Al-Hayat*. "I have spoken about this in order to warn the youth against them, youth who are seduced by them, and don't know them." (Dr Fadl's rebuke was so damaging to al-Qa'ida's reputation that Ayman Zawahiri felt compelled to publish a two-hundred-page rebuttal of his former mentor.)

Yet whatever military success the United States and its allies have had in disrupting al-Qa'ida's operations and destroying its cells has been hampered by the failure to recognize and confront the social movement—Jihadism—of which al-Qa'ida is merely the most militant manifestation. The truth is that al-Qa'ida has always been less an entity than a system of thought, a "mode of activism," to quote Abdullah Azzam. "Al-Qa'ida is not an organization," declared Abu Musab al-Suri. "It is not a group, nor do we want it to be. It is a call, a reference, a methodology." Though the word "al-Qa'ida" is almost always rendered in English as "the base"—something concrete and conquerable, something that can be defended or assailed—"al-Qa'ida" more properly means "the rules" or "the fundamentals" and is used by Arabic speakers primarily to refer to the basic teachings or creed of Islam. In that light, it may be somewhat appropriate to consider al-Qa'ida a form of Islamic fundamentalism, insofar as that word implies puritanical adherence to the elemental doctrines of a religion. But it would be imprecise, even dangerous, to consider al-Qa'ida the operational seat of Global Jihadism. Indeed, as a transnational social movement, Jihadism has no operational seat.

For al-Qa'ida, the wars in Iraq and Afghanistan have become central fronts in what bin Laden calls a "Third World War, which the Crusader-Zionist coalition began against the Islamic nation." Yet while these wars have no doubt provided Jihadist ideologues with an invaluable recruiting tool, one perhaps on a par with the occupation of Palestine, for those Muslim youths who identify with Global Jihadism as a social movement there is no central front to the War on Terror because their identity cannot be confined to any territorial boundaries. Rather, theirs is a transnational identity linked together not by language, ethnicity, or culture but by a set of grievances—both local and global, real and imagined—that has created a shared narrative of oppression and injustice at the hands of the West. These are young, mostly middle class, politically active, and socially conscious Muslims who, while they may consider al-Qa'ida to be the only force in the Muslim world giving voice to their grievances, are nevertheless unlikely to actually take up arms and join the jihad (though, as we shall see, with the right mixture of incentive and indignation, they can be coaxed into action).

The threat of terrorism from militant groups like al-Qa'ida may never fully dissipate. As is the case with any international criminal conspiracy, it may take years, perhaps decades, of cooperation among the military, intelligence, and diplomatic apparatuses of nation-states around the globe to put an end to their activities. But to adequately confront the social movement that Osama bin Laden and Ayman Zawahiri inspired a decade ago will require more than military might. It will require a deeper understanding of the social, political, and economic forces that have made Golbal Jihadism such an appealing phenomenon, particularly to Muslim youth. Whatever the War on Terror means, this is an ideological battle that will take place not in the streets of Baghdad or in the mountains of Afghanistan but in the suburbs of Paris, the slums of East London, and the cosmopolitan cities of Berlin and New York. It is a battle that will be waged not against men with guns but against boys with computers, a battle that can be won not with bullets and bombs but with words and ideas.

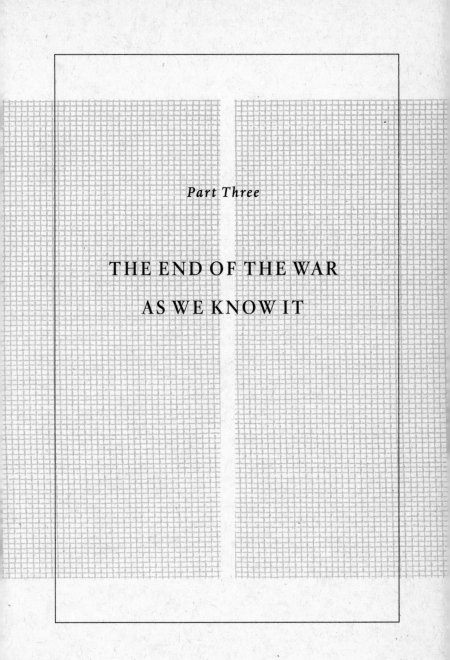

*Part Three*

# THE END OF THE WAR
# AS WE KNOW IT

# CHAPTER SIX

# Generation E

There is no more deliriously frenetic airport in all of Europe than Heathrow. Its five broad terminals stretch across miles of low-lying greenbelt in West London and take in more international traffic than any other airport in the world. If there were an axis around which all air travel spun, Heathrow would be it. Indeed, Heathrow is less an airport than a cosmopolitan village: a Babel of exotic faces and unfamiliar tongues; a blaring, boisterous jumble of people elbowing their way from one end of the world to the other.

I arrive at Heathrow at the crack of dawn, the fog in my mind as thick and turbid as the fog that unfurls on the tarmac as we hit the runway. There is no immigration officer to pull me aside as I disembark, so I am free to catch a ride with the other passengers pushing their way through the dips and bends of Terminal 3—a few of us branching off every now and then to other, unseen terminals—until we are all, at last, deposited at passport control.

It is hard not to notice how the more globalization has eroded our borders, the more ostentatious the policing of those borders has become: the labyrinthine queues, the firm-faced officers, the eager dogs, the color-coded signs, the stalls that trap and herd passengers along like cattle. This is all a matter of security, of course. But it is also a matter of control—or rather, the illusion of control. In a world in which national boundaries are becoming increasingly irrelevant, there is some comfort in knowing that here, at the edge of our fast-fading territorial frontiers, the state still maintains a measure of control, not over identity, perhaps, but at least over to whom it does or does not grant entry.

There is a difference between Heathrow and some other airports, however. Look up and you see it: two distinct paths for travelers to take. The first is marked for visitors like myself; we wait patiently in a long line that snakes around a metal maze to be properly identified and registered as "Guests of the United Kingdom." The second path, marked with a ring of golden stars on a shiny blue square, is not just for British citizens, as one might expect, but for "Citizens of the European Union." Those who take this route—whether French or Spanish or German or Dutch or Latvian or Swedish or Romanian or Maltese or any one of twenty-seven separate nationalities—need barely slow down as they flash their matching passports at the sleepy immigration officer slumping in his cell. For the citizens of these nation-states, passing from one country in Europe to another is a bit like strolling from neighborhood to neighborhood.

Freedom of movement among the citizens of Europe is not a new phenomenon. Europeans have trod on one another's lands, spoken one another's languages, eaten one another's cuisine, and shared one another's cultures for centuries. But the creation of the European Union (EU) has transformed this gaggle of sovereign states, which a mere sixty years ago nearly brought the continent to ruin, into what Winston Churchill liked to call "the United States of Europe."

The European Union is an unprecedented geopolitical realignment the likes of which has not been seen since the end of the Roman Empire. How remarkable that a group of independent states, united by nothing more substantive than geography, would agree to band together under a single constitution and a common court, a single currency and a common market: one parliament, one passport, one birth certificate, one citizenship, one community made up of twenty-seven sovereign states (and counting), with twenty-three languages and half a billion members. A continent without borders.

For enthusiasts of globalization, the European Union offers a thrilling glimpse into a future of transnational interdependency. Its creation signals a rejection of the politics of exclusion that dominated so much of the previous century and an embrace of a singular global civilization. In the eyes of a new, borderless generation of Europeans, whom the writer T. R. Reid calls "Generation E" and who "consider themselves not as Spaniards or Czechs but rather as Europeans who happen to be living in Toledo or Prague," the EU serves as the beau ideal of the global peace and prosperity that may be possible if nation-states join together in friendship and cooperation to promote their common interests.

For critics of globalization, the European Union is a nightmare of unfettered capitalism, cultural dilution, and, ultimately, the loss of national identity. Over the last decade, as it has forged ahead with a slew of treaties and referenda to bind member states together more fully under a federal system (and to bring ever more members on board), a wave of xenophobia and ultranationalism has swept through Europe. Hence the sudden success of a host of unabashedly racist right-wing political parties such as the French National Front, the British National Party, and the Freedom Party of Austria, or the mainstream appeal of neofascist politicians such as France's Jean-Marie Le Pen, Geert Wilders in the Netherlands, or the late Austrian agitator Jörg Haider.

The appeal of these parties and politicians derives from their ability to tap into the widespread fear among many Europeans of globalization and its consequences: the curbs on national sovereignty, the new configurations of power, the unfamiliar bureaucracies, and, most of all, the alien and exotic faces that have suddenly become part of the cultural fabric of their once homogeneous landscapes. All of this has made Euro-skepticism a much more common phenomenon throughout Europe, even among Generation E. In 2005, both France and the Netherlands, two of the European Union's founding states, rejected an EU draft constitution by wide margins. Not coincidentally, that same year, bloody riots tore through France's immigrant ghettos, engulfing Clichy-sous-Bois and several other Paris suburbs. A year earlier, a Moroccan immigrant named Muhammad Bouyeri butchered the controversial filmmaker and professional provocateur Theo van Gogh on the streets of Amsterdam, a city in which nearly half of the population is of foreign origin. These two events, followed by fiery protests over the Danish newspaper *Morgenavisen Jyllands-Posten*'s publication of the Muhammad cartoons, which were almost immediately reprinted in newspapers and magazines across Europe in a show of "solidarity," further inflamed a continentwide debate over what it means to be French or Dutch or Danish in an increasingly heterogeneous, increasingly borderless Europe. All of this has provided cover for ultranationalists to present themselves as the defenders of ethnic and cultural unity— nationalism's bone and marrow—against the barbarian hordes washing up on Europe's shores with the rising tide of globalization.

Of course, in today's Europe, the barbarian hordes happen to be mostly *Muslims*. In fact, the massive surge of Muslim migration into Europe over the last fifty years has created a situation in which Europe's identity crisis being experienced almost wholly through the lens of Islam. It seems that the Muslim has replaced the Jew as Europe's new "negative pole."

To be sure, Islam has always played a pivotal role as Europe's quintessential Other. The borders of what we know today as Europe were established in large part through the continent's encounter with Islam—from the shifting battle lines of the Crusades to the defense of the Hapsburg Empire against the Turks. But the deterritorialization of Europe has altered the equation, making it impossible to separate Europe's turbulent relationship with Islam from the larger questions of sovereignty and national identity that have arisen as a direct result of globalization. So, for instance, in France, the refusal to serve halal meat to Muslim kids in school cafeterias has become what Olivier Roy has called a matter of "territorial reconquest" for French nationalists, a means of exerting "national cohesion by asserting a purely political identity that confines to the private sphere any specific religious or cultural identities." In Germany, the construction of new mosques has been halted by political and civic leaders who argue that the buildings are not places of worship but "symbols of a parallel world." The Netherlands has introduced legislation to ban the Qur'an, which some politicians claim conflicts with "Dutch values." In the United Kingdom, the Muslim veil has been denounced as "a mark of separation" by former prime minister Tony Blair and veiled women condemned as "a walking rejection of all our freedoms." No matter that less than 3 percent of Muslim women in the U.K. wear the veil. The point is that the veil and the mosque and Muslim dietary requirements have all become unmistakable signs of Islam's *otherness,* the most obvious and most convenient foil for an aggressive and suddenly revived European national identity. Visit any of the dozen or so large, ethnically isolated enclaves one finds throughout Europe—say, the British working-class town of Beeston in southern Leeds, two hundred miles north of Heathrow—and one thing becomes perfectly clear: fear of Islam in Europe goes hand in hand with fear of globalization.

Beeston was once a thriving factory and mill town, but the factories and mills are now mostly closed. Their burnt-out stacks loom over the city like warped minarets. The city is divided into two areas—Beeston Village, a bucolic, mostly white working-class neighborhood of charming Victorian homes and new shopping centers, and Beeston Hill, the run-down neighborhood to the east of the Village, which is now home to the majority of Beeston's Muslim population.

In Beeston Hill, at almost any hour of the day, one can find groups of unemployed teenage boys, mostly first- and second-generation Pakistanis, loitering in back alleys smoking cigarettes. There are jobs in Beeston: as one resident told me with a bitter smile, "The call centers are always hiring." But most of the kids work in family shops, where they can at least earn enough money for cigarettes and chips, until one day they're in their twenties and realize that all they have is cigarettes and chips. And so they turn to drugs or Islam.

The families in Beeston Hill are close-knit. There is no choice. This is a dense residential area. Some of the dilapidated redbrick housing units are shaped like a horseshoe, with a fenced-in weed garden in the middle. Satellite dishes perch on every balcony. Two, maybe three families—usually from a single village in Pakistan—may share a house: the white sheets hanging on the line in the front yard could be anyone's sheets; the old, bearded men entering and leaving the houses in their slippers and *shalvar kameez* could be anyone's uncles. Community is the rule here.

By the British government's own admission, the standard of living in Beeston Hill is among the worst in Britain. There is poverty, drugs, gangs—everything one finds in any forgotten, depressed neighborhood. There is also stark, in-your-face, matter-of-fact racism.

ISLAM OUT OF BRITAIN!

The words, scrawled on the wall of a local pub, are like a punch in the stomach. I do not know what to make of them until a friend informs me that this was the slogan of a popular leaflet campaign launched by the right-wing British National Party (BNP). For years, the BNP had been bellowing about the creeping "Islamification" of Britain. But after 9/11, its xenophobic platform, which, among other things, calls for a ban on all Muslims flying into or out of the United Kingdom, as well as a boycott of all Muslim-owned businesses ("Not those owned by Chinese or Hindus," a BNP publication helpfully clarifies, "only [those owned by] Muslims as it's their community we need to pressure"), suddenly found a receptive audience in the United Kingdom. (A YouGov/Sky News Poll in 2006 showed that nearly 60 percent of British citizens believed that all further immigration into the United Kingdom should be halted.) The party that in 1990 was described by the European Parliament as "openly Nazi" has today become a legitimate force in British politics, managing in 2006 to more than double its number of council seats, from twenty to forty-six. By 2008, that number had risen to one hundred.

The rise of the British National Party coincides with a rise in anti-EU sentiment throughout the United Kingdom. The BNP has become a receptacle for Euro-skepticism of all stripes, the party that has most obviously benefited from Britons' fears of globalization (on the BNP website, the EU flag is represented with a golden swastika in the middle of the ring of stars). At the same time, the BNP's success in the most recent elections is a direct result of the party's sudden and single-minded focus on what it terms the "Muslim problem."

Standing with my friend in the drizzle, reading those angry and determined words on the wall of the pub, it dawns on me that this is not the first time I have encountered BNP propaganda. On July 12, 2005, five days after the Jihadist attacks on the London Underground and bus system, a BNP flier was distributed around the country depicting the mangled, burned-out husk of bus number 30, which was destroyed in a suicidal blaze by Hasib Hussain, the youngest of the 7/7 bombers. At the bottom of the flier was a brusque yet pointed message: "Maybe it's time to start listening to the BNP."

Hasib Hussain, like his fellow 7/7 bombers, Mohammed Siddique Khan and Shehzad Tanweer, was born in West Yorkshire and grew up right here, among Beeston's large Muslim community (the fourth bomber, Jermaine Lindsay, was a convert and recent immigrant from Jamaica). The youngest of four children, Hasib came from a tight-knit, though not unusually devout, family. His father and mother (both British citizens), his brother, and his sister-in-law shared a comfortable four-bedroom home in the district of Holbeck. Several more members of his extended family lived nearby.

The Hussains were not poor, not by Beeston standards. Hasib's father had a steady job working in a factory. His brother was a successful administrator in Leeds. Hasib was not a particularly bright kid. He was not particularly zealous or particularly idealistic. He was unremarkable in almost every way, which is why his friends and family, and even the British authorities, were so baffled by his sudden murderous turn. Yet as it turns out, this unexceptional and unassuming second-generation Pakistani-Briton from West Yorkshire was the prototypical

Jihadist. In fact, the path that young Hasib Hussain took from shy teenager to the bomber of bus number 30 is so well trod that his life provides the perfect template for understanding the phenomenon of Global Jihadism as a social movement.

First a few words about social movements and the role that religion so often plays in shaping and nurturing them. Social movements arise when relatively powerless people band together under the banner of a collective identity in order to challenge the existing social order. Such movements are, almost by definition, utopian in character, in that they are fervently engaged in reimagining society. This is particularly true of so-called transformative social movements, such as Global Jihadism, which seek a complete upending of the old social order through violent revolution, often in anticipation of cataclysmic global change.

Social movements are by no means a modern phenomenon, as demonstrated by the Zealots. Nor are they strictly secular, as evidenced by the evangelical movement. However, it was the advent of modernity that empowered social movement members to so radically reimagine the nature of human society. Modernity, of course, is a tricky term to define. The concept tends to be associated with issues such as mass urbanization and rapid industrialization as societies transitioned from feudalism to capitalism. But one can argue that the hallmark of the modern age is the sudden shift in human consciousness that occurred when people began to realize that the accepted norms and values of society were not fixed or absolute, let alone divinely mandated, but rather man-made and malleable. In other words, with modernity came the recognition that society was merely a human construct, one that could be rapidly and profoundly altered by individuals working in solidarity with one another.

Just as modernity altered the way individuals understood their relationship to society at large, so did it fundamentally change the way individuals understood themselves. It used to be that a person's identity was defined by the society to which he or she belonged. But as society was increasingly deemed to be nothing more than the product of human imagination, so too were social identities cast aside as mere human constructions. After all, if there are numerous alternatives to the present social order, there must also be numerous alternatives to the identities that society ascribes to us. Thus, with the rise of modernity, new collective identities began to arise, constructed not through societal mandates but through conscious self-reflection—not "Who do you say I am?" but "Who do *I* say I am?" In short, the modern age has ushered a transition from a world in which identities were bestowed to a world in which identities can be gained or lost through deliberate action—from a world of ascribed identities to a world of self-identification.

This shift in consciousness is usually traced to the beginning of the nineteenth century, an era that witnessed the first organized challenges to the accepted social order. The French Revolution (1789–1799) in particular, with its rallying cry *"Liberté, égalité, fraternité,"* permanently upended the time-honored orthodoxies of human society, not just in France but throughout Europe, as large groups of individuals began mobilizing, first loosely and defensively, then more organized and offensively, in response to the massive social changes taking place throughout the industrialized world. These individuals were not just challenging the accepted social order; they were questioning its very foundation. Why should the world be as it is? Why should it not be different? Why not dramatically so?

Such utopian ideals have led more than a few social scientists to dismiss social movements as the refuge of the malcontent. To this day, some social movements—the black power and feminist movements of the 1950s and '60s, for example, or the radical environmental or antiglobalization movements of today—are viewed as nothing more than short-lived, unstructured, and extreme reactions to societal stress, spurred by individuals unmoored by the natural changes of society: a herd of cattle in a state of alarm.

The problem with this perception is that it ignores the very real grievances at the heart of social movements. The environment really is deteriorating. Globalization truly does destroy indigenous economies.

Blacks, women, the marginalized and dispossessed do often suffer at the hands of the powerful and elite. That some social movements seek to address these grievances, not through the long slog of political participation or legal reform but through sweeping societal change (or in the case of a transnational social movement such as Jihadism, *global* change), does not necessarily make them irrational or deviant, no matter how disruptive their actions may be to a society's accepted social norms. As the sociologist Michael Schwartz wryly noted, participants in social movements are just as rational as those who study them.

The perception of social movements changed in the 1960s, primarily in response to the legitimate countercultural challenges posed by racial and ethnic groups, student groups, environmental groups, and others, all of which sought to create broad cultural, social, and political shifts in society through organized, collective action. These days, social movements are more or less universally viewed as "normal, rational, institutionally rooted political challenges by aggrieved groups." Yet there is still enormous reluctance among some sociologists to expand the definition of such movements to include groups that, while functioning exactly like a social movement, choose to define themselves in explicitly religious terms. Perhaps this is because scholars are used to thinking of religion as an isolated field of study, one too often brushed aside by the secularization theories that dominated sociological studies throughout much of the twentieth century. But in this new, emerging century, as the boundaries between religion and politics are, in all parts of the world, becoming increasingly blurred, we can no longer afford to view religious movements as inherently different from any other group of individuals who have linked their individual identities together with the purpose of challenging society.

The truth is that religion has certain qualities that make it a particularly useful tool for promoting social movement activism. Religion can tap into a person's deeper sense of self—the existential self—giving members a profoundly personal and emotional stake in the success of the movement. At the same time, religion brings to a social movement the hierarchal structures, financial resources, communication channels, and manpower that are so vital in getting the movement off the ground. A huge part of the success of the civil rights movement in the United States came from its ability to use black churches as venues for disseminating information from the pulpit to the streets.

Social movements must provide participants with certain "selective incentives" to convince them that they have something to gain from joining. When religion is involved, these incentives become easier, since people of faith are usually willing to sacrifice earthly rewards for the promise of a heavenly one. And one must not forget that those who claim the mantle of religious leadership, even if they are not offi-cially recognized by their religious institutions (indeed, especially if they are not recognized by their religious institutions), tend to enjoy an automatic sense of authority and legitimacy that would otherwise take years for social movement leaders to develop on their own. Think of the leftist priests who led Latin America's Liberation Theology movement, many of whom were excommunicated by the Vatican for doing so (Pope John Paul II referred to them as the "internal enemy" of the Church). It was the collars they wore around their necks, not the guns they carried in their belts, that drew to these priests an army of the poor and dispossessed.

Or consider bin Laden, a man with no religious credentials who has never studied in any Islamic seminary and who has only the most rudi-mentary knowledge of Islamic law and theology, but who has never-theless managed to seize for himself the powers traditionally ascribed to Islam's clerical class by, for example, repeatedly issuing his own fat-was (which, according to Islamic law, can be issued only by a qualified member of the clergy). It is his conscious appropriation of religious authority that has made bin Laden so appealing to those Muslims—particularly young European Muslims like Hasib Hussain and his fel-low 7/7 bombers, who are themselves mostly ignorant of Islamic law and theology—whose sense of alienation from their own religious communities makes them yearn for alternative sources of spiritual leadership. In his speeches and writings, bin Laden warns these young Muslims not to listen to their clerics, whom he considers incapable of addressing their needs. "No official scholar's juridical decrees have any value as far as I'm concerned," he has declared. In fact, bin Laden makes the astonishing claim that following the leadership of these "hypocrite imams" (by whom he means any member of the clergy that disagrees with his interpretation of Islam) is "tantamount to worshiping [them] rather than God." He then audaciously takes upon himself the duty, traditionally reserved for Islam's clerical class, of "enjoining what is right and forbidding what is wrong." It is a clever manipulative trick: convince young Muslims to stop obeying their religious leaders while assuming for yourself those leaders' religious authority.

We have already seen how a social movement relies on the use of symbols to create solidarity among members across ethnic, cultural, linguistic, and national boundaries. For such symbols to be effective, they must be familiar enough to be recognized and easily absorbed by the movement's members, yet new enough to arouse excitement and interest; they must reflect societal values while also challenging them. Religion, with its familiar yet infinitely malleable supply of symbols, provides a reservoir of ready-made symbols—words, phrases, and images—that can be interpreted and reinterpreted as often and as innovatively as one likes to invest a movement's message with meaning and significance. So, for example, zeal can be a symbol of personal piety or pious revolt. The cross of Christ can be employed as both an emblem of peace and a banner of war. Jihad can simultaneously be an internal struggle against sin and an external struggle for liberation. These symbols can be appropriated from traditional religious authorities and recast in such a way as to draw a sharp distinction between the old, outmoded, arcane, and apolitical posture of the temple, the church, or the mosque and the new, innovative, populist position represented by the social movement.

Finally, and most significantly, religion's ability to sanction violence, to declare it permissible and just, to place it within a cosmic framework of order versus chaos, good versus evil, is indispensable to the success of a social movement. As the sociologist Sidney Tarrow writes, there can sometimes be no more effective means to simultaneously "weld supporters together, dehumanize opponents, and demonstrate a move-ment's prowess" than through an act of organized collective violence.

Violence can be as essential an element in religion as love, charity, or any other aspect of the human condition. Unless a religion aspires to nothing more than metaphysical contemplation, it has no choice but to contend with society's other "group-forming mechanisms"—ethnicity, culture, politics, nationalism—all of which (like religion) cre-ate boundaries between in-groups and out-groups, and all of which (like religion) regularly employ violence in doing so. The intersection of religion and violence over time and across cultures has less to do with the logic or substance of religion itself than with the fact that both religion and violence function as durable markers of collective identity: the simplest, most effective means of saying who is *us* and who is *them*.

Religion, of course, can be just as effective in promoting nonvio-lence and civil disobedience, as was the case with America's civil rights movement or India's movement for independence from Britain. But for movements that operate in societies where democratic institutions are either wholly absent or brutally repressed by the ruling regime, countries where legitimate opposition is simply not allowed, collective violence may be the sole means for a social movement to pursue its goals of radical social transformation, as Latin America's Liberation Theology movement discovered.

Developed by a handful of politically active priests throughout the 1970s and 1980s, Liberation Theology relied on familiar Christian sym-bols and metaphors (the Eucharist, the suffering of Christ, the coming of the Kingdom of God) to unite the impoverished and downtrodden of Latin America under a single collective identity and encourage them to rise up and challenge the accepted social order. By casting Jesus as a poor, illiterate revolutionary who fought the ruling powers of his time on behalf of the oppressed and marginalized, Liberation Theology sought to redefine the Gospel story in purely sociopolitical terms, as a means of fighting back against the ruthless, U.S.-backed regimes in countries such as Nicaragua, El Salvador, and Guatemala.

Yet when these regimes responded to the Liberation Theology movement with indiscriminate and unrestrained state-sanctioned violence, when soldiers began raping and murdering nuns with impunity and executing priests during Mass, when it became clear that the international community would do nothing to curb the brutality (Ronald Reagan actively supported the actions of these regimes, calling Liberation Theology "a threat to U.S. national security"), the Christian revolutionaries felt they had no choice but to turn to violence themselves. As Father Ernesto Cardenal, who joined the Sandinista revolution in Nicaragua, bluntly declared, "[Christ] says we must love the enemy, but he doesn't say we can't fight them. . . . Christ forbade the sword but not the machine gun."

These were shocking words for many Christians, particularly those living comfortable, middle-class lives in the peaceful suburbs of North America and Western Europe. But as Archbishop Oscar Romero, perhaps the most famous of the countless martyrs of Latin America's Liberation Theology movement, argued, if there can be no peace without justice, and if justice must sometimes be fought for, the Church "cannot simplistically say it condemns any kind of violence."

"We know," Romero wrote in an epistle to the Church, "how the great number of peasants, workers, slum dwellers, and so forth, who have organized themselves to defend their rights and promote legitimate structural changes, are simply judged to be 'terrorists' and 'subversives' and so are arrested, tortured, made to disappear, or are murdered, with no law or judicial institution to protect them or to give them a chance to defend themselves and prove their innocence. Faced with these uneven and unjust odds, they have often felt forced to defend themselves, even with violence."

It is important to recognize that the kind of violence Romero refers to is organized, ritualized violence: *sacred* violence. As Mark Juergensmeyer notes, the Christian revolutionaries in Nicaragua, El Salvador, and Guatemala did not perceive their struggle for freedom from oppression as merely a political conflict but rather as a cosmic contest between the absolute forces of good and evil, a conflict in which God was actively engaged on behalf of the poor and dispossessed against the wealthy and powerful, a conflict in which everyone must pick a side. "Either you are with the slaughtered or you're with the slaughterers," cried Father Cardenal.

But though violence can be an integral part of a social movement, if taken too far, it can become a liability, as we have seen with Jihadism. On the one hand, violence can create the perception that change is possible, thus convincing people with similar grievances to align themselves with the movement one way or another. And as certain tactics, such as suicide bombing, begin to show success, they are picked up by other members of the movement. On the other hand, violence can lead to even greater repression by the state, which in turn can further radicalize the movement and thus frighten away sympathizers and invalidate the movement's grievances. This is the great paradox of social movements, whether religiously inclined or not: the more violent the reaction to the movement, the more violent the movement may become. What ultimately led to the deradicalization of the Liberation Theology movement—or, for that matter, the environmental movement, the antiglobalization movement, the feminist movement, the black power movement, and so on—was the gradual co-option of their members' grievances into mainstream society. Indeed, when it comes to dealing with a social movement, society has only two options: either it can address the members' grievances, thereby making the movement irrelevant, or it can deflect those grievances and further radicalize the movement. Or as Sidney Tarrow puts it, "actions that begin in the streets [can be] resolved in the halls of government or by the bayonets of the army." The challenge facing many European governments when it comes to dealing with Global Jihadism is whether to pursue greater force or greater accommodation. Which approach they choose will dictate whether Jihadism in Europe gradually becomes insignificant or instead festers within Europe's immigrant communities long enough to explode into full-scale revolution.

———

There are more than twenty million Muslims in Europe, the majority of whom are immigrants from former European colonies. Indeed, immigration throughout much of Europe is, for a host of reasons, inextricably linked to the unsettling process of decolonization. Hence, the majority of immigrants in the United Kingdom—including Hasib Hussain, Mohammed Siddique Khan, and Shehzad Tanweer—are from South Asia (India, Pakistan, Kashmir), while in France most immigrants hail from former French colonies like Morocco and Algeria.

Starting in the 1950s, a wave of migrant workers from the Middle East and North Africa swept into Europe, mostly to clean up the devastation of World War II. Many of these workers had little contact with government entities, as they were for the most part recruited and employed by private firms and housed in ethnically segregated hostels and guesthouses. These were poor, mostly young men, isolated from the rest of European society, who created their own insular communities based on the languages, religions, or cultures they had in common. They maintained deep ties with their home countries and regularly sent their paychecks back to their wives and children. Few had any intention of making a permanent home in Europe.

After the oil embargo in 1973 caused a crisis in the global economy, leading to massive job losses throughout Europe, immigration laws were tightened. Many countries now required "proof of personal connection" to be allowed legal entry. Yet far from curbing immigration, the new laws launched a second wave of migration into Europe, as the wives and children of migrant workers, worried that they would forever be separated by the new legal restrictions, began flooding into the continent to join their husbands and fathers.

The reunification of immigrant families, particularly in urban areas such as Leeds, Berlin, and Rotterdam, fostered a far greater sense of conservatism and a deeper emphasis on religious observance among Europe's Muslims. Islam became a means of maintaining family cohesion in a foreign and unfamiliar land. Little by little, large ethnic enclaves began popping up throughout Europe: in Beeston Hill; in

Berlin's Kottbusser Tor, dubbed "Little Istanbul," whose garbage-choked streets are lined with row upon row of dilapidated housing complexes, nondescript kebab shacks, Turkish newsstands, Arab markets, and the occasional sex shop; in the heart of Rotterdam, where a quarter of the population is from either Turkey or Morocco.

From Britain to Brussels, one often hears dire warnings about the impending takeover of Europe by these Muslim immigrants. It is a widespread fear fueled by a barrage of bestselling books with histrionic titles such as *Londonistan, While Europe Slept,* and *The West's Last Chance*—the last written by the right-wing journalist Tony Blankley, who warns that "the threat of the radical Islamists taking over Europe [today] is every bit as great . . . as was the threat of Nazis taking over Europe in the 1940s." It is difficult to take such hysterical comments seriously, considering that Muslims make up 2 to 4 percent of Europe's total population and demographers do not expect that number to rise far beyond 6 percent. Yet research done by sociologist Marc Sageman shows that over the past few years 84 percent of those who have actively participated in the Global Jihadist movement were first- or second-generation immigrants, living mostly in Europe. That is a startling statistic, and it has led some to conclude that the rise of radical Islam in Europe is due primarily to a lack of integration. Muslims, it is argued, must be made to assimilate fully into European society in order to keep them from falling into the trap of Jihadism. They must become secularized and Westernized. They must learn Europe's languages and fully adopt Europe's customs. They must align their mores and values with those of their new home. Otherwise, they must return to their old ones.

The problem with this argument is that most Muslims living in Europe are already fairly well integrated into European society. European Muslims, especially second- and third-generation immigrants, speak European languages, take European university degrees, and live by and large as Europeans. Islam in Europe has so thoroughly absorbed European ideals of religious and cultural pluralism, of individualism and human rights, of liberalism and modernity that scholars often speak of a wholly new and culturally distinct form of European Islam, which Bassam Tibi calls "Euro-Islam."

Even a fundamentalist, antidemocratic organization such as Europe's arm of the Hizb ut-Tahrir—a Salafist organization that, despite its rejection of violence, nevertheless seeks to re-create the global Caliphate—is, ironically, supremely European in its posture and perspective: it employs the language of European civil rights, demands the political freedoms and privileges afforded to it by the European Constitution, speaks almost exclusively in European tongues, and relies on the fundamental principles of European civil society to freely preach a message that would lead to prison and torture of its members were they to try the same in their fathers' countries. The members of Hizb ut-Tahrir who rally against British foreign and domestic policy in universities throughout the United Kingdom, who march and hold seminars propagating their religio-political beliefs, are doing so, whether they recognize it or not, as children of the Enlightenment. It is *Europe* that most clearly informs their political ideology, not Islam. In fact, the world they seek—a world without borders—is the world in which they already live. The European Union is the model of the global Caliphate.

In any case, lack of integration is hardly an issue for Europe's Jihadists. Hasib Hussain was, by all accounts, well integrated into British society, as was the leader of the 7/7 attacks, Mohammed Siddique Khan, a beloved schoolteacher known to his non-Muslim friends as "Sid." Jamal Zougam, the man thought to be responsible for placing the explosions on a Spanish commuter train that killed 191 people on March 11, 2004, was a fairly successful businessman in Madrid. Ahmed Omar Saeed Sheikh, the murderer of *Wall Street Journal* reporter Daniel Pearl, was a highly educated British-born Pakistani from a well-adjusted middle-class family.

These men are doctors, lawyers, and engineers, the best and brightest of their communities, the pride of their immigrant families. They are precisely the kind of well-educated, socially conscious people who tend to flock to social movements: people who have the material and mental resources to mount collective challenges to the accepted social order. Jihadism attracts the same kind of person who, in other circumstances and with different challenges, would have joined an antiglobalization or civil rights movement. That Jihadists like Hasib Hussain are extreme in their views and violent in their tactics does not take away Jihadism's legitimacy as a social movement. As Tarrow writes, "Extremism is an exaggerated form of the frames of meaning that are found in all social movements . . . [just as] violence is an exacerbation of collective challenges."

Hasib was an average student, more interested in sports than in his studies, but he did finish high school and go on to earn a degree in an advanced business program. Neither he nor any other 7/7 bomber was a product of a madrassa—one of the Islamic schools that, in Europe and North America, are often viewed as terrorist factories where young Muslim children are trained to hate "the infidel." Worldwide, only about 13 percent of Jihadists have had any kind of religious education (not a single 9/11 hijacker attended a madrassa), which makes sense, considering that madrassas tend to be the reserve of the poor, who cannot afford any other kind of education. And if there is one thing that Jihadists—whether in Europe or in the Middle East—have in common is that they tend not to be poor.

True, Muslim immigrants in Europe live at economic levels far below those of most of their fellow Europeans. Poverty breeds resentment. It breeds hopelessness. And both of these can be used as effective recruitment tools for Jihadist leaders. Still, it is a well-documented fact that the majority of those who turn to Global Jihadism are, like Hasib and his mates, from middle-class families.

Hasib Hussain, Mohammed Siddique Khan, and Shehzad Tanweer all worshiped at the Stratford Street Mosque in Beeston. But as the official British report on the attacks of 7/7 makes clear, Hasib's indoctrination into Jihadism occurred away from the mosque, away from all places with any known links to extremism. It is ironic that the bulk of European governments' antiradicalization efforts has been focused, almost myopically, on mosque surveillance—since 2002, the German police have raided more than three hundred mosques, with little to show for their efforts than the resentment and distrust of Germany's Muslim population—because Jihadists do not gather in mosques. Hasib actually met Khan and Tanweer not at the Stratford Street Mosque but at the Hamara Healthy Living Centre, a popular youth club in Beeston where Khan ran an outreach program. Not even the infamous Finsbury Park Mosque in North London, where the Jihadists Richard Reid and Zacarias Moussaoui worshiped and where for a brief time the *takfiri* enthusiast Abu Hamza al-Masri served as imam (al-Masri was publicly sacked by the mosque's board and is currently in prison for inciting racial violence), turned out to be the Jihadist breeding ground 'it was made out to be in the press. Neither the 3/11 cell in Madrid nor the 9/11 cell in Hamburg had any connection to a mosque.

The modern Jihadist network can be likened to a self-organized, sometimes spontaneous, informal group of close friends who tend to come together away from their own religious communities ("bunches of guys," Marc Sageman calls them). This is what the official British investigation of 7/7 meant when it concluded that, "group identities, formerly rooted in nationalist causes, became less important whilst loose networks of individuals, often centered on a leading figure, became more commonplace." At most, the mosque serves as a place where certain disaffected kids, those who may feel marginalized and out of place in their communities and who may therefore be susceptible to the message of jihad, can be identified.

Hasib's sudden turn to radical Islam came not through contact with his mosque but after a trip to Saudi Arabia in 2003. He began praying more often and wearing traditional Pakistani clothes. He talked about becoming an imam. Yet his newfound piety was underdeveloped and unsophisticated, which made him the perfect target for a proudly anti-intellectual, anti-institutional movement such as Jihadism. Part of the appeal of Osama bin Laden as a spiritual leader is that he is seen as untainted by the traditional clerical establishment, the *ulama*. Bin Laden, you will recall, is not a cleric and has no religious training. In his speeches and declarations he routinely refers to the traditional Muslim clergy as "imams of infidelity," "defeatist imams," or "hypocrite imams" ("Our so-called scholars," in the words of Mohammed Siddique Khan). When bin Laden declared that the 9/11 hijackers had rejected all conventional schools of law in favor of the law of the Prophet Muhammad, he was not suggesting that they were simply good and faithful Muslims, followers in the path trailed by the Messenger of God. He was in fact mocking the privileged status of the *ulama* as the exclusive interpreters of the law. "Don't you dare associate with those [*ulama*] who follow their own whims and desires, who are a burden on the earth," bin Laden warns his followers, "or those who have bowed before the oppressors, spreading lies about you, and holding you back from this blessed jihad."

Because Jihadism cannot compete intellectually with the traditional *ulama*, it is compelled to deny the very authority upon which the law and practice of Islam are founded. This subversive rejection of Islamic law and clerical precedent in favor of a direct, unmediated experience of faith, in which every believer is an imam, is incredibly attractive, especially in Europe, where young Muslims are already distanced from the traditional institutional centers of their religion and where "vernacular" forms of Islam dominate the religious landscape.

And make no mistake, it is *kids* that Jihadism seeks. Sageman's research indicates that the average age of Jihadists detained by the European and Canadian governments is twenty. Hussain was just eighteen years old when he died, which in bin Laden's eyes made him the perfect candidate. "We find that the only age group capable of giving and waging jihad is the fifteen to twenty-five age bracket," he has stated. "I instruct the young people to exert every effort in jihad, for it is they upon whom this duty primarily devolves."

These youths tend to show little interest in the arcane and often painfully out-of-touch sermonizing of their imams. They find traditional, conservative interpretations of Islam unsatisfying. They are hungry for a more intimate spirituality that cannot be contained by the walls of the mosque, and, as with most religiously inclined social movements, they form their collective identities *in direct opposition* to the formal religious authorities of their community. When it comes to religious instruction, they are mostly self-taught. They rarely understand Arabic, are not educated in Islamic law, and tend to be suspicious of those who do have Islamic credentials. They consider too much intellectualism as spoiling the emotional immediacy of their simple and unconditional faith. And because in Europe they generally have greater access to education and mass communication technologies, because they have been saturated with European ideals of individualism, they are far more likely than their coreligionists in Arab and Muslim majority states to prefer self-styled spiritual gurus to traditional imams and to abandon clerical precedent for "self-actualization." They are, in a word, *European*.

Only they are rarely made to feel so, either by their fellow citizens or by their governments. Although far more integrated into Europe than their parents, first- and second-generation Muslim youths tend to feel even more excluded from European society, precisely because their expectations and their sense of entitlement are greater. The historically restrictive citizenship laws of many European countries— often based on the law of *jus sanguinis* (right of blood), whose purpose is to maintain a measure of ethnic homogeneity by linking nationality to ethnicity—have made it difficult for immigrants to feel like equal members of society. For example, a person of Turkish descent who was born in Germany, whose father was born in Germany, whose grandfather was born in Germany was until recently not automatically considered a German citizen. (The laws were reformed in 1999 to make it easier for immigrants to apply for citizenship.) Europe's anti-discrimination laws are equally restrictive, in that they provide legal protection only for ethnic or racial groups and not for religious communities. Though some laws have recently been extended to include so-called monoethnic religious groups, such as Sikhs and Jews, multi-ethnic religious groups, such as Muslims, Jehovah's Witnesses, and Rastafarians, are not afforded the same level of legal protection from religious discrimination. In fact, in Italy, Muslims are not even officially recognized as a religious community (despite being the largest religious minority in the country), meaning they are severely hampered by laws pertaining to the construction of religious buildings and the distribution of federal taxes.

To make matters worse, new antiterrorism laws throughout Europe have resulted in what some human rights groups term "institutional discrimination." Such laws have poisoned relations between religious groups and law enforcement officials so that young European Muslims often bluntly admit that they would not cooperate with the police under any condition for fear of being "databased," that is, put under surveillance themselves.

Many of these youths feel they are living in a continent in which discrimination and Islamophobia are becoming increasingly mainstream, and the European Monitoring Center on Racism and Xenophobia agrees. In a 2006 report, the Vienna-based organization concluded that physical attacks, acts of vandalism, and discrimination against Muslims in both the job and housing markets have surged to unprecedented levels throughout Europe. (A survey by the Allensbach Meinungsforschungsinstitut, for instance, found that 83 percent of Germans equate the word "Islam" with terrorism.) A large proportion of Muslims interviewed for the study felt that their acceptance into European society was predicated on the assumption that they should "lose their Muslim identity," that they could be either Muslim or European but not both.

This was exactly the challenge faced by Hasib Hussain. Like most of his peers, Hussain (as well as Tanweer and Khan) made numerous visits to Pakistan to visit family. And like most of his peers, he found that he had little emotional connection to the country or culture of his parents. A former member of Hizbut-Tahrir in Britain put the dilemma of many Muslim youths in Europe this way: "When I went to Pakistan I was rejected. And when I came back to Britain, I never felt like I fitted in to the wider British community. And you've got to remember that a lot of parents didn't want us to fit into the British community."

The crisis of identity faced by these young Muslims, many of whom feel they belong in neither the West nor the East, drives them to seek out new identities that cannot be contained by any culture or society, that in fact reach across all boundaries of race, ethnicity, and nationality. That is, they seek a deterritorialized identity to match the deterritorialized world in which they live. And they find that identity online. Indeed, thanks to the Internet, the worldwide community of faith that the Jihadists have long envisioned has become a virtual reality.

The Internet allows Jihadist leaders to conduct sophisticated media campaigns aimed at communicating their message to a global audience. Al-Qa'ida even has its own media wing called as-Sahab, which produces and distributes a daily stream of media content, from high-quality propaganda videos and documentaries dubbed into multiple languages to audio recordings and statements by bin Laden and others. The videos often depict images of Muslims around the world suffering at the hands of Western aggression. These images are spliced together with successful Jihadist attacks against enemy targets in places like Iraq and Afghanistan, creating a master narrative in which the Jihadist fighters are seen as the saviors of besieged and oppressed Muslims around the world.

Although the Internet provides Jihadist leaders with an invaluable tool for communication, it is debatable what role their online offensive actually plays in radicalizing Muslim youths. (The official British inquiry into the 7/7 attacks concluded that there was little evidence that Khan, Tanweer, and Hussain were big Internet users.) That is because the overwhelming majority of participants in social movements comprise what sociologists refer to as "free riders"—people who share the movement's grievances, who associate with the movement's goals, and who have absorbed the movement's symbols into their own identities, but who do not take part in the movement's actions. In the case of Global Jihadism, free riders are those who join chat room discussions and download Jihadist videos but who are attracted to Jihadism as they would be to any other antiestablishment movement—casually, and as a form of rebellion. Theirs is a "pop-culture Jihadism," akin to the radical student movements of the 1960s, the punk rock subculture of the late 1970s, or the grunge "anticulture" movement of the 1990s. It boasts its own style of dress, its own slang, its own symbols of conformity, even its own music—rap and heavy metal songs glorifying jihad against the *kafir.* These kids may don the Palestinian kaffiyeh, or national headscarf, in fellowship with a people with whom they have no connection. They may wear Osama bin Laden T-shirts as though he were a modern-day Che Guevara or pin his poster to their walls as if he were a soccer superstar; they may identify with the grievances of the Global Jihadist movement and feel a sense of solidarity with the plight of Jihadist militants around the world. But to mobilize these youths and encourage them to move beyond mere collective identity and toward collective action requires a prolonged personal connection with active members of the movement that can be difficult to sustain. (This explains why it often takes an undercover agent posing as a member of al-Qaʻida to infiltrate these so-called bunches of guys and compel them to action.)

A prolonged personal connection is precisely what turned Hasib Hussain from a dissaffected youth into a Jihadist suicide bomber. Mohammed Siddique Khan's position at the Hamara Healthy Living Centre afforded him the opportunity to seek out and identify possible candidates such as Hussain for indoctrination into Jihadism, though the actual indoctrination took place away from any public space, privately, by way of sustained personal contact and intensive group bonding. Sociologists maintain that there are three necessary steps to incite social movement activism. First, question the legitimacy of the present social order. Then make people believe that the social order can be overturned. And finally, convince them that their active participation is crucial to the movement's success. According to the official British report, these steps perfectly mirrored the mobilization techniques employed not only on the 7/7 bombers but on Muslim youths throughout Europe.

First, the potential recruit is identified as someone who may be susceptible to the Jihadist message. In Berlin, reports have surfaced of Jihadist leaders posing as parents and attending "parent-teacher conferences" at schools where they can probe into which students are doing poorly, who is having trouble integrating, who may be expelled, and so on. Once identified, the recruit is exposed, through the Internet and satellite television, to the widespread injustices faced by Muslims around the world. Islam's traditional religious and political leaders are revealed to be corrupt and complicit in the plight of these oppressed Muslims; they are the Near Enemy—hypocrites and apostates to be avoided. International conflicts involving Muslim peoples—whether in China, Kashmir, Chechnya, Afghanistan, or Iraq—are presented as part of a larger "war against Islam," led by an imperial, crusading West (the Far Enemy), which only the Jihadist militants fighting on Islam's behalf have the courage or power to repel. Examples are offered of the miraculous successes these fighters have had in battling the world's great superpowers, both past (the Soviet Union) and present (the United States and Israel), demonstrating that change is possible, that, with the right actions, the world can be remade.

This may be sufficient to urge certain disaffected youths to become involved in Global Jihadism as a social movement, but it is not enough to mobilize them to action. Mobilization occurs only when the global grievances to which they have been exposed are connected to the local grievances that they themselves experience every day as outsiders who lag far behind their fellow Europeans when it comes to employment opportunities, legal representation, civil rights, and educational advantages; as outcasts who are constantly scrutinized by the media and by politicians who accuse them of disloyalty to the state; as foreigners forbidden to express their cultural and religious identity because of legal bans against head scarves or restrictions on the construction of mosques; as immigrants demonized not only by right-wing parties but by mainstream European society; as pious young men and women hectored and humiliated by pseudointellectuals such as Aayan Hirsi Ali, Oriana Fallaci, and Brigitte Gabriel, who make a living fanning the flames of racism and Islamophobia.

Thus, when the French legislature passed a law prohibiting young Muslim girls from wearing head scarves (*hijab*) in public schools, in a deliberate attempt to assert a cohesive national identity upon its citizenry by forcefully excluding from the public realm any individual religious or cultural identity (a practice the French term *laïcité*), Ayman Zawahiri issued the following communiqué to his followers across the globe: "Banning the *hijab* in France is consistent with the burning of villages along with their people in Afghanistan, demolishing houses over their sleeping residents in Palestine, and killing children in Iraq and stealing its oil under false pretexts. . . . It is consistent with tormenting prisoners in the cages of Guantanamo and torturing Muslims in the prisons of our leaders, the friends of the United States."

Only after a master frame has been firmly established, wherein an injustice to any Muslim in the world is perceived as an injustice to them (and vice versa), are the theological doctrines of Jihadism introduced. Only then is their world cleanly divided between the oppressed and the oppressors, the slaughtered and the slaughterers, the good and the evil: *al-wala' wal-bara'*. Only then does the recruit begin to believe that offensive jihad against innocent civilians and his fellow Muslims is justified. Once he has been stripped of his individual identity and fully assimilated into the collective, only then is the recruit offered the option of suicide terrorism as a legitimate act of war and, more important, a viable means of vengeance for his people.

The perception of the suicide terrorist is that he is driven by hatred toward his target or by a lack of value for life. But as Marc Sageman has argued, "It is actually quite difficult to convince people to sacrifice themselves just because they hate their target. . . . On the contrary, it appears that it is much more common to sacrifice oneself for a positive reason such as love, reputation, or glory."

Hasib Hussain stepped aboard bus number 30 in pursuit of radical global transformation. He was not coerced into committing his awful crime; he was not brainwashed. He was a zealot, acting alone and without guidance from anyone save God; he was a knight, called by God to renew his faith by shedding the blood of unbelievers; he was a martyr, sacrificing his own life for the lives of "his people." It may have been anger and humiliation and a deep-seated feeling of inequity that led Hussain to Global Jihadism. But it was love that made him a suicide bomber—imprudent, misguided, confused, and misplaced love. Love fueled by a romantic notion of jihad as a cosmic war fought on God's behalf, by a juvenile belief that the world can be remade with just a few pounds of explosives.

Not long after the London attacks, I went to Beeston Hill to try to speak with Hasib's friends and family. At the time, few in the community would accept that young Hasib had been involved in the attacks. "We are decent people," Hasib's father cried in a heartbreaking interview in the London *Independent.* "I worked hard all my life. Please, please, please don't say it's something to do with me or that I knew, my son knew, my wife knew. We are very, very decent people. I think it must have been somebody else on the bus. Not Hasib. He was a good boy." Some in the neighborhood argued that Hasib had been manipulated by the leader of the group, Mohammed Siddique Khan. Many desperately clung to rumors swirling around the community that the 7/7 bombings had been "an inside job," a deliberate attempt to trigger an anti-Muslim backlash in the United Kingdom, "a way to finally push us out of the country," as one Beeston resident told me.

When I returned to the neighborhood some years later, the residents of Beeston Hill had more or less resigned themselves to accepting Hasib's guilt and the guilt of his coconspirators, though their sense of disaffection and marginalization had only increased in the wake of the 7/7 bombings, the public discussions that had ensued over the compatibility of Islamic and European values, and the debates in the media about whether membership (read, citizenship) in the European Union requires immigrants and the children of immigrants to strip away their cultural affinities and their "communitarian attachments" to their race, religion, and ethnicity in order to sufficiently assimilate into European society.

What I found was that a great many of Europe's young Muslims are becoming increasingly frustrated by what they consider to be unreasonable and inconsistent demands for them to fully subsume their Muslim identity into the national identities of their adopted countries.

(Many feel that having religious values of any kind makes them out-casts in Europe.) The majority of European Muslims with whom I spoke claimed they had already done all they could to integrate into European society and honestly had no idea what more was expected of them. "I was born here," a second-generation German Muslim from Turkey told me, "I speak German. I even have a Ph.D. I follow the laws. I accept the Constitution. What more do they want from me? What must I do to finally become German? Just tell me, and I'll do it." When I posed this question to a political studies professor at Germany's pres-tigious Universität Tübingen, he paused for a long moment before an-swering with a shrug. "There is no such thing as *becoming* German. You either are or you are not."

That statement, more than any religious or cultural or socioeco-nomic considerations, accounts for why Global Jihadism has become so appealing to Europe's young Muslims. If in the face of globalization and the rapid deterritorialization of the continent the native popula-tions of the European Union are having a difficult time defining their individual national identities, how much more arduous must that task be for immigrants and the children of immigrants? How can one fully participate as an equal member in civil society if membership is predi-cated on identifying with the dominant culture? The simple fact is that in a country wherein civic identity is difficult to define, where ethnicity and nationality are considered to be one and the same, a foreigner will remain a foreigner forever.

It is within such "identity vacuums" that Global Jihadism thrives. For kids like Hasib Hussain, whose religious and cultural affinities have been cast by their societies as *other*, Jihadism is more than an alternative form of identity—it is a *reactionary identity*, a means of social rebellion. It is an identity formed through the deliberate linking of local and global grievances—both real and perceived—to create a single, shared narrative of suffering and injustice. And only by severing that link, and disrupting the narrative, can Global Jihadism be defeated.

The first part of that process has already begun throughout much of Europe. In the United Kingdom, the government has begun placing far greater emphasis on addressing the socioeconomic obstacles, not to mention the religious and racial discrimination, that have kept a great many Muslim immigrants from feeling like equal members of British society. Nationality laws have been revamped so as to develop a more universal, more easily accessible conception of British national identity. Immigrants seeking citizenship in the United Kingdom must now demonstrate sufficient language skills, as well as become adept in British history, culture, and national customs. All of this is an attempt to construct a collective identity based not on ethnic or cultural homogeneity but on a common national narrative, one in which every member of society can share. (Similar programs are under way in France, Spain, Italy, and Germany, though at a much slower pace than in the United Kingdom).

Thus far, the response from Muslim leaders to these reforms has been overwhelmingly positive. There has been almost unanimous support from groups such as the Muslim Council of Britain—the largest and most active of Britain's Muslim organizations—for new government initiatives requiring foreign imams who wish to work in the United Kingdom to be proficient in English. This seemingly simple gesture has had an enormous impact on the relationship between Britain's religious leaders and the country's young Muslims, allowing mosques and Islamic centers to reframe themselves as community hubs where kids can take part in the kinds of social programs that were once the sole purview of community centers like the Hamara Healthy Living Centre, where young Hasib Hussain first met Mohammed Siddique Khan. Meanwhile, a slew of British Muslim organizations, including the Federation of Student Islamic Societies, the Al-Furqan Islamic Heritage Foundation, and the Quilliam Foundation (a counterextremism think tank founded by former members of Hizbut-Tahrir), have set about defining a uniquely British conception of Islam, which has allowed a new generation of Muslim youth to feel increasingly comfortable exerting both their national and their religious identities.

These reforms have already begun to have an impact on Muslim integration throughout Europe. But they are only the first step in confronting Global Jihadism. It is not enough to merely address the local grievances of Muslims. Global grievances, bound up as they are with local grievances, must also be addressed. And in this regard, only the United States, which remains the most dominant economic and military power in the world, can change the narrative between Islam and "the West." This is true not only because the United States is at the forefront—militarily, economically, politically, and culturally—of the conflict between Europe and North America on the one hand and Muslim majority states on the other, but also because, as the embodiment of the freedoms of faith and conscience for which all peoples of the world strive, America is itself the most powerful weapon against the spread of Global Jihadism.

Much has been written about why Muslims in the U.S. have, for the most part, managed to avoid many of the problems of identity and integration facing Muslim communities in Europe. Obviously, economic circumstances have played a significant role: While the majority of Muslims in Europe hail from impoverished immigrant families, the majority of Muslims in the United States are solidly middle-class. The median income for a Muslim household in America is slightly greater than it is for a non-Muslim household, and American Muslims have one of the highest rates of literacy and education of any immigrant group. And certainly America's long and storied history of absorbing different cultures, religions, and ethnicities has made a difference in shaping the experience of American Muslims. According to demographers, America—already the most racially, ethnically, and religiously diverse country on earth—will soon become the only country wherein minorities form the majority.

But undoubtedly the most significant factor in allowing American Muslims to comfortably reconcile their faith and traditions with the realities of American life is the core American belief that there need be no conflict between one's religious and nationalist identities. Above all else, it is America's commitment to the freedoms of religion, and religious expression, that has made Muslims in the United States so much more resistant to the pull of Jihadism than their European counterparts. And it is precisely that same freedom that continues to draw Muslims from all over the world to the promise of the United States. Having traveled throughout the Middle East, I have experienced firsthand how the idea of America as a sponge that absorbs whatever faith, culture, or ethnicity it comes into contact with can overcome the often irresistible pull of anti-Americanism. I have watched Muslims chant "Death to America!" on the streets of Tehran, then privately beg me to help them get a visa to the U.S. Despite the way in which the War on Terror has poisoned America's image across the Muslim world, even America's staunchest critics still recognize that there is no country—and certainly no Islamic country—in which Muslims can pursue their religion with more freedom and openness than in the United States.

Of course, with all of this comes the enormous responsibility of placing the very ideals at the heart of the American experience—pluralism and democracy, sovereignty and the rule of law—at the center of U.S. foreign policy, *come what may*. As we shall see, this is certainly the case when it comes to dealing with Islamist groups like Hamas, Hizballah, and the Muslim Brotherhood. Reaching out to such groups will by no means be an easy task. But, in the end, it is the only way to truly become "the light among nations."

# CHAPTER SEVEN

# The Middle Ground

The American University in Cairo (AUC), with its manicured lawns and—considering the parched surroundings—inexplicably lush gardens, is situated in the heart of Midan Tahrir, or Independence Square, but it might as well be in another world, so disconnected is it from the rest of boisterous Cairo. Inside the university's fortified walls, Egypt's moneyed boys and girls are instilled with the ideals of a Western liberal education. (The school was founded by Americans in 1919 for just this purpose.) The AUC is also a hub for foreigners studying Arabic abroad. I myself honed my Arabic skills there in the summer after the attacks of 9/11. At the time, the school had become a favorite of American military students who journeyed to Cairo for a crash course in the language of the enemy. Here, close-cropped future soldiers would learn how to introduce themselves to strangers, the proper way to order a falafel and a Coke, how to shout *Get out of the car! On your knees!*—and, as I heard practiced over and over again in the halls of my hotel that summer, how to say "freedom" in Arabic: *hurriya.*

I tried to steer clear of the military students, not because I was troubled by their presence—on the contrary, I was relieved to know they would have some language skills before being handed a thin pamphlet illustrating the five pillars of Islam and shipped off to war. Rather, it was because during the first few days of instruction, whenever one of them ran into me in the lobby he would ask for fresh sheets or new towels, apparently confusing me with the cleaning boy. After a few awkward encounters they made a point of avoiding me altogether, and I returned the favor.

Between classes at the AUC, there was little to do but sit with the unemployed Egyptian men in the cafés, under the shade of a tattered canopy, slowly sipping sweet mint tea as the sun inched its way across the lichen-colored sky. By then, no one talked about anything else except the war in Afghanistan, the war everyone knew would be coming to Iraq, and America's "crusade against Islam." The conversations that shot from table to table tended to avoid me as if I were an innocent trapped in a firefight. Once or twice I leaned in toward an onslaught of words to ask a well-rehearsed question in my most flawless Arabic. But I was always answered in French or English, and with a sneer. How did they know I was American?

I began wearing a knitted skullcap and dark sunglasses, as though I carried my identity in my eyes and only by hiding them could I join these conversations. But despite the darkness of my skin and the conformity of my dress, the men knew instinctively that I was not one of them. (The irony of the Americans assuming I was Arab, and the Arabs assuming I was American, was not lost on me.) Slowly, it dawned on me that my country had given these men the same simple ultimatum it had given me: if you are not with us, then you are with the terrorists. And whatever their loyalties or political persuasions, however they felt about America and its policies in the region, however much they may have detested al-Qa'ida and its abhorrent actions, one thing was absolutely, undeniably clear. *They were not with us.*

Inside the AUC, where the conversations were mostly in English, the talk was all about the late Samuel Huntington's book *The Clash of Civilizations and the Remaking of World Order,* which, though published several years before, had become a surprise bestseller in Cairo. Huntington had argued that the fundamental source of conflict in the twenty-first century, particularly when it came to the West and the Islamic world, would be neither ideological nor economic, but civilizational. "The fault lines between civilizations will be the battle lines of the future," he wrote almost a decade before the attacks of 9/11.

The Egyptian students at the AUC loved the book, if for no other reason than it seemed to them that Huntington had placed "Islamic civilization" on par with "Western civilization" in his imagined global clash, but also because the thesis appeared to confirm what the Jihadists had been saying for years. "This [clash of civilizations] is a very clear matter," Osama bin Laden told a television reporter for Al Jazeera in October 2001. "[It is] proven in the Qur'an and the traditions of the Prophet, and any true believer who claims to be faithful shouldn't doubt these truths, no matter what anybody says about them."

In the United States, Huntington's thesis almost instantly formed the philosophical backbone of the War on Terror. It was as though Americans needed to place the events of 9/11 into an easily accessible drama—one in which every historical actor had a role to play—and the drama that seemed most suited to the American psyche at the time began with a classic Sophoclean prologue: two unseen forces—"Islam" and "the West"—hurtling toward each other in a catastrophic yet inevitable collision, determined by the gods long before but hidden from the eyes of men until, in an explosion of light and sound, both suddenly appeared on stage.

Few stopped to ask the most basic question of this ill-conceived theory, namely, what is meant by "Islamic civilization" (or, for that matter, "Western civilization")? Does it refer to the cultural traditions of the Arab world, whose inhabitants make up 10 percent of the globe's 1.5 billion Muslims? Perhaps it means Persian civilization, which despite dominating much of Islam's early evolution reaches back a thousand years before the birth of the Prophet Muhammad and has little in common with Arab culture? Or maybe it is a reference to the Mongol Empire, which swallowed the whole of the Middle East in the thirteenth century, or the Turkish Ottoman Empire, whose norms, ethics, aesthetics, and ideals prevailed over much of the Muslim world for the seven centuries that followed?

The truth is, none of these distinctive cultures is meant when referring to "Islamic civilization." The term does not signify any specific cultural, societal, or governmental state reached by any group of Muslim peoples in any place or time. It has no meaning at all, save for some exotic abstraction through which an imaginary "Western civilization" can more easily define and contain an equally imaginary "Islamic civilization," setting one in opposition to the other. Indeed, if the phrase "Islamic civilization" means anything at all, it means simply "Islam," just as "Western civilization" has become a kind of shorthand for Christianity. Huntington himself admitted as much. "The underlying problem for the West is not Islamic fundamentalism," he wrote in his influential book. "It is Islam."

By transforming the countless cultures of the Arab and Muslim world—from Morocco to Malaysia—into a single, homogeneous, and historically inevitable enemy, the Clash of Civilizations, insofar as it has served as the ideological underpinning for the struggle against Jihadism, is a blatant assertion that the War on Terror is in fact a war against Islam. After all, this was never conceived of as a war against terrorism per se. If it were, it would have included the Basque separatists in Spain, the Christian insurgency in East Timor, the Hindu/Marxist Tamil Tigers in Sri Lanka, the Maoist rebels in eastern India, the Jewish Kach and Kahane underground in Israel, the Irish Republican Army, the Sikh separatists in the Punjab, the Marxist Mujahadin-e Khalq, the Kurdish PKK, and so on. Rather, this is a war against a particular brand of terrorism: that employed exclusively by Islamic entities, which is why the enemy in this ideological conflict gradually and systematically expanded to include not just the persons who attacked America on September 11, 2001, and the organizations that supported them, but also an ever-widening conspiracy of disparate groups such as Hamas in Palestine, Hizballah in Lebanon, the Muslim Brotherhood in Egypt, the clerical regime in Iran, the Sunni insurgency in Iraq, the

Chechen rebels, the Kashmiri militants, the Taliban, and any other organization that declares itself Muslim and employs terrorism as a tactic. According to the master narrative of the War on Terror, these are a monolithic enemy with a common agenda and a shared ideology. Never mind that many of these groups consider one another a graver threat than they consider the West to be, that they have vastly different and sometimes irreconcilable political yearnings and religious beliefs, and that, until the War on Terror, many had never thought of the United States as an enemy in any war.

No wonder, then, that nearly 80 percent of Muslims around the globe came to believe that the United States seeks to "weaken and divide the Islamic world," while almost two thirds thought the purpose of the War on Terror is to "spread Christianity in the region." In every Muslim majority state in the world, positive perceptions of the United States reached an all-time low, even among its staunchest allies. According to a 2006 poll by the Pew Global Attitudes Project, 70 percent of Egyptians, 70 percent of Indonesians, 73 percent of Pakistanis, 85 percent of Jordanians, and 88 percent of Turks (all U.S. allies) held an unfavorable view of the United States. If the War on Terror was meant to be an ideological battle for the hearts and minds of Muslims, there should no longer be any question that the battle has been lost.

It did not have to be this way. When then–Secretary of State Condoleezza Rice journeyed to Egypt in 2005, she stood before the assembled students and faculty of the American University in Cairo and made a startling admission. "For sixty years," she said, "my country, the United States, pursued stability at the expense of democracy in this region here in the Middle East—and we achieved neither. Now, we are taking a different course. We are supporting the democratic aspirations of all people." This was a remarkable statement, one that flew in the face of half a century of American foreign policy in the Middle East.

Rice was heralding a loosely organized set of foreign policy principles dubbed "the Bush Doctrine," which among other, more perilous

propositions (for example, the principle of preventative war), put forth
the radical notion that the policy of the United States should be "to
seek and support the growth of democratic movements and institutions in every nation and culture, with the ultimate goal of ending
tyranny in our world." As Bush himself declared during his second inaugural address, "All who live in tyranny and hopelessness can know:
the United States will not ignore your oppression, or excuse your oppressors. When you stand for your liberty, we will stand with you."

Promoting democracy in the Middle East was neither a new nor an
innovative idea. Past administrations had pressed for political and social reforms throughout the region. But what Bush seemed to be suggesting was a transformational project in which the promotion of
democracy would form the foundation upon which relations between
the United States and the Muslim world would henceforth be based.

Perhaps for that reason, Bush was roundly ridiculed both in the
United States and abroad. Most of the American media dismissed his
florid democracy rhetoric as little more than an attempt to legitimize
the invasion of Iraq. The Arab press, too, mocked Bush's democracy
project as inauthentic and hypocritical—an excuse to wage unending
war throughout the Muslim world under the pretext of spreading
"freedom" and "liberty." Bush's promise to stand with democratic reformers "facing repression, prison, or exile" was thought to be a joke,
considering that these reformers were facing their persecution at the
hands of America's dictatorial allies—Egypt, Jordan, Saudi Arabia, and
Morocco—all of which had spent decades convincing the Western
powers that even the slightest weakening of their regimes would result
in the immediate takeover of the Middle East by radical Islamists.

Still the Bush Administration pushed ahead, pressuring Egypt's
president, Hosni Mubarak (who had succeeded Anwar Sadat), to consent to having members of the banned Muslim Brotherhood take part
in parliamentary elections. (Mubarak also agreed to hold Egypt's first
contested presidential election, allowing the dissident political activist
Ayman Nour to run against him.) The administration pressed the

Lebanese government to hold elections that resulted in a greater role in government for Hizballah. And, in what was perhaps its most inspired move, the administration gave Palestinians their first chance to choose their own political leaders in free and fair elections.

For a brief while, it seemed that the political sands might be shifting across the Middle East, as "power in the world's least democratic region [was] at last beginning to pass from long-ensconced rulers to their restive subjects," to quote *The Economist*. Despite widespread apprehension toward the United States and deep hatred for George W. Bush in particular, there was a genuine feeling on the Arab street that a new narrative might be written about the relationship between the United States and the Muslim world, one where America was cast not as Crusader but as champion of the dispossessed. Large majorities throughout the region told pollsters that they believed the United States truly wanted to see the Muslim world move toward democracy. A few months after the president's second inaugural speech, Gallup International found that 78 percent of people in the Middle East considered democracy "the best form of government." One year later, in 2006, a Pew poll found that while the majority of the Western public thought democracy was "a Western way of doing things that would not work in most Muslim countries," pluralities or majorities in every single Muslim country surveyed flatly rejected that argument and called for democracy in their own countries. In Algeria, Yemen, Tunisia, Bahrain, Jordan, Morocco, even Saudi Arabia, a wave of democratic fervor resulted in unprecedented political challenges to the authoritarian regimes of those countries. The sense of excitement and opportunity brought scores of people who had spent their lives in autocratic societies to the polls to choose, even if in the smallest of ways, their political destinies.

The results were astounding. In Lebanon, Hizballah picked up an impressive fourteen seats in the parliament—three more than its previous total—as well as two cabinet positions. In Jordan, the Islamists of the Islamic Action Front, an offshoot of the Muslim Brotherhood, won

15 percent of the seats in parliament. And, of course, in Palestine, Hamas trounced its political rival, Fatah, and took control of the Palestinian Authority.

Yet it was in Egypt, the cultural capital of the Arab world and the country in which Condoleezza Rice first announced the Bush Doctrine to the region, that the experiment in democracy promotion was most visibly put to the test. In spite of violent repression from Mubarak's security forces, who beat and shot voters, closed down polling booths, and randomly imprisoned opposition leaders, members of the Muslim Brotherhood, running as independent candidates, managed to gain 88 of the 444 seats in Egypt's parliament, essentially becoming the country's first legitimate opposition party.

Like Islamist parties in Morocco and Turkey, which had also made the transition from banned opposition groups to legitimate members of the government, Egypt's Muslim Brotherhood quickly realized that the responsibilities that came with working within the government (rather than opposing it from without) left little room for radical ideologies. Far from trying to transform Egypt into a theocracy, as Arab rulers across the region had warned it would, the Brotherhood fully embraced the opportunity of political participation by creating alliances with liberal intellectuals and secular democrats in the parliament. Brotherhood members lobbied the regime for greater political freedoms, including freedom of religion, assembly, and speech. They formed coalitions with other opposition groups, and even with members of Mubarak's own National Democratic Party, to try to bring an end to three decades of the emergency rule, put in place in the aftermath of Sadat's assassination, that had allowed Mubarak to rule the country with an iron fist. These actions for the first time transformed the sclerotic Egyptian parliament into something akin to an actual legislative body. Gradually, the Muslim Brotherhood convinced even its staunchest critics that, given the opportunity, it could become a legitimate political force in Egyptian politics. And precisely for that reason, Mubarak turned the full force of the police state against them.

In a series of aggressive moves meant to consolidate his power and

push back against the increased popularity of the Muslim Brotherhood, Mubarak canceled municipal elections, forced a package of constitutional changes through parliament (despite a vigorous boycott by
the Brotherhood and its allies), rounded up thousands of lawyers,
judges, journalists, and political opponents, including Ayman Nour,
the liberal democrat who had run against him in the presidential elections, and threw them all in jail.

The world held its breath, waiting for a cue from the United States
as to how to respond, not just to Mubarak's sudden crackdown but
also to the sweeping political changes that were taking place throughout the region. There was, understandably, enormous apprehension
on the part of leaders both in the United States and around the globe
about recognizing militant groups such as Hamas and Hizballah,
whose ideological platforms so blatantly contradicted American interests in the region. However, there was also a sense that if the Muslim
Brotherhood could succeed in transforming itself from an opposition
movement into a political party, perhaps it could provide an example to
other Islamist groups to put down their weapons and pick up ballots
instead.

The answer the world had been waiting for came with Secretary
Rice's subsequent visit to Cairo the following year, in 2006. Standing
next to Mubarak, she praised him for his "democratic" reforms, making no mention of either the canceled elections or the arrests of
Mubarak's opponents. Later, after Rice was already on her way back to
Washington, Mubarak boasted that the secretary "didn't bring up difficult issues or ask to change anything or to intervene in political reform. . . . She was convinced by the way that political reform and the
implementation of democracy are being done in Egypt." In fact, Rice
had come to Cairo for only one purpose: to persuade Mubarak to join
Europe, the United States, and Israel in cutting off all aid to Hamas as
a means of forcing it out of power in Palestine.

The message was clear. By refusing to engage the democratically
elected leaders in Lebanon and Palestine, and by looking the other way
as its allies in Jordan, Egypt, Morocco, and Saudi Arabia reverted to

their despotic behavior, the United States was telling the world that the promise of peaceful political reform through democratic participation was a lie. As it turned out, this was precisely the message that Ayman Zawahiri had broadcast to the Muslim world in a videotaped speech lambasting the Muslim Brotherhood, Hamas, Hizballah, and other Islamist groups for trusting the United States in the first place and taking part in elections. "Anyone who calls for Islam while presenting [a system of] infidelity, such as democracy . . . is a *kafir*," Zawahiri wrote in his widely circulated book, a critique of the Muslim Brotherhood entitled *The Bitter Harvest: The Brotherhood in Sixty Years*. "Whoever claims to be a 'democratic-Muslim' or a Muslim who calls for democracy . . . is a *kafir*."

It would not be an exaggeration to say that the experience of "democracy," as it has been so clumsily promoted these past few years, has created widespread hostility throughout the Middle East not only toward the United States but toward democracy itself. The very word "democracy" has been tainted by the blatant hypocrisy and diplomatic bungling of the Bush administration; by the transformation of the War on Terror into a cosmic war; by the extent of anguish, misery, loss, and death that have resulted from the wars in Afghanistan and Iraq; by the bald violation of American values and ideals in the pursuit of al-Qa'ida militants; by the reversal of American pledges to support freedom and self-determination come what may; by the unfulfilled aspirations for social and political reform in the Middle East. Indeed, for many in the region, democracy has become a byword for chaos and conflict; at best, a bland euphemism for regime change.

But while the policies of the previous American administration only strengthened Jihadism and increased its appeal, particularly among Muslim youth, there is at last an opportunity to start anew in America, to throw off the shackles of the past few years and reformulate the ideological conflict against radical Islam. Eight years after George W. Bush presented the world with a stark ultimatum—"Either you are with us, or you are with the terrorists," he warned a few days after the attacks of September 11, 2001; "in this conflict there is no neutral ground"—the election of Barack Hussein Obama has changed the equation in the Middle East and utterly transformed the perception of the United States among Muslims. From the beginning, indeed from the very first moments of his presidency, President Obama has made it his mission to actively and aggressively engage the citizens of Muslim majority states through the language of mutual respect. (A lack of respect is cited as the prime reason by the overwhelming majority of Muslims when asked what they see as hindering relations with Western countries.) "My job is to communicate to the American people that the Muslim world is filled with extraordinary people who simply want to live their lives and see their children live better lives," Obama declared in an interview with the Arabic news channel Al Arabiya—the first interview he gave as president. "My job to the Muslim world is to communicate that Americans are not your enemy."

Obama's words are more than a repudiation of the clash-of-civilizations mentality. They are seemingly an effort to make himself—the son of a Muslim father from Africa and a Christian mother from Kansas—the bridge linking Islamic and the Western civilizations together as one. And they have left Jihadist ideologues like Ayman Zawahiri and Osama bin Laden scrambling to find some response to an American president who can proudly proclaim, "I have Muslim members in my family. I have lived in Muslim countries."

Yet while the new American president should be praised for discarding the religiously polarizing rhetoric and cosmic worldview of the previous administration in his attempts to forge a new relationship with a part of the world that has all too often been demonized by Americans, he must not abandon his predecessor's albeit clumsy and blundering efforts to promote democracy in the Middle East, not if the grievances that continue to buttress Global Jihadism are to be sufficiently addressed. For example, in his historic "Address to the Muslim World" in Cairo in June of 2009, Obama spoke movingly of the daily humiliations of the Palestinians, referring to the situation in the Palestinian territories as an "occupation," a word no other American president has dared to use. But he barely made mention of democracy and had very little to offer beyond the barest of platitudes for the one issue that poll after poll in nearly every Muslim majority state indicates is the biggest concern of Muslims: the lack of political rights. Tellingly, the few words he did have on the topic of democracy received the loudest and most sustained applause from the audience in the hall, an indication that this is a topic that Obama cannot afford to ignore.

The fact is that on this one issue, President Bush was right: only through genuine democratic reform can the appeal of extremist groups be undermined and the tide of Muslim militancy stemmed. But this task will require more than showy speeches and empty promises. It will require vigorous and sustained pressure on U.S. allies in the region (that is, those nations that receive billions of American dollars in economic and military aid every year) to concede to the growing demands of their populations for a voice in government, to put a stop to arbitrary imprisonments and the silencing of political opponents, and to allow for greater political participation, especially by religious nationalist groups that are willing to commit to responsible governance. Indeed, despite the blame heaped upon Bush's democracy promotion for the increased violence and instability that has gripped much of the Middle East, particularly in Lebanon and Palestine, the solution to peace and prosperity in the region remains more democracy, not less.

There are obviously risks in pushing political reform in such a volatile region. One could argue that the war between Israel and Lebanon in 2006 (sparked by a Hizballah attack on an Israeli army patrol) and the subsequent war between Israel and Hamas in the Gaza Strip are both prominent reminders of the dangers of promoting democracy in this part of the world. "Is Arab Democracy Worth All This Chaos?" asked a headline in the online journal *Slate*. Undoubtedly, some of the governments that will arise from truly democratic elections in the Middle East may hold views and pursue policies that are contrary to the interests of the United States. But so long as the ruling regimes in these countries ignore the demands of their people (with the tacit approval of the United States) while Islamist groups like the Muslim Brotherhood, Hamas, and Hizballah work to address their socioeconomic needs, populations throughout the region will continue to throw their support behind the Islamists—as well they should. It is a political truism that when it comes to elections, he who cleans the streets gets the votes. Rather than make it impossible for people to elect Islamists, perhaps we should give them reason *not* to.

In any case, whatever risks there may be in promoting democracy in the Middle East, they pale in comparison to the risks involved in continuing to stifle political reform in the hope of achieving stability in the region. Terrorism thrives in societies where no public space exists for legitimate political opposition. As we saw with the Liberation Theology movement, when peaceful voices are silenced, violence becomes the sole source of political expression. Throughout the Middle East, whenever moderate Islamist parties have been allowed to participate in the political process, popular support for more extremist groups has diminished. Consider the case of Turkey's Justice and Development Party (Adalet ve Kalkınma Partisi, or AKP), the wildly popular Islamist party that heads the Turkish government. The AKP's transformation from a banned opposition group into a powerful political force—one that has brought Turkey back from the edge of fiscal collapse, improved ties with Israel and the United States, and granted the country's oppressed Kurdish minority greater freedoms—has virtually sapped the country's more radical religious groups, such as the Great Eastern Islamic Fighters Front and the Islamic Liberation Movement, of any popular support. Conversely, when Islamist opposition has been suppressed, militant groups and religious extremists have gained favor. The Algerian Civil War, which ravaged that country for nearly a decade in the 1990s, is a strong case in point: the rise of an ultraviolent Jihadist organization, the Armed Islamic Group (GIA) in Algeria was the direct result of the government's decision to ban political participation by the more moderate Islamists of the Front Islamique du Salut (FIS).

Islamism, in other words, can act as a foil to Jihadism. Unlike Jihadists, whose aims and aspirations rest on a cosmic plane, Islamists have material goals and legitimate ambitions that can be addressed by the state. Whereas Jihadists view political participation as an act of apostasy, Islamist parties throughout the Middle East have shown that, given firm political rules to abide by and a fair chance to govern, they can evolve into responsible political actors committed to democratic ideals of human rights, women's rights, government accountability, the rule of law, pluralism, and judicial reform. Predictions that electoral victories by Islamist parties would inevitably result in the demise of democracy have thus far proven false. In fact, whenever people in the Middle East have had an opportunity to choose between more moderate and more radical Islamist positions, they have consistently sided with the moderates. (It should be noted that, for all its violent actions and inflammatory rhetoric, Hamas is actually the more moderate and accommodating of the Islamist groups in Palestine, particularly when compared to its bitter rival, the Palestinian Islamic Jihad.) Even in Pakistan's North-West Frontier Province, the base of al-Qa'ida and the Taliban and likely the place where bin Laden and Zawahiri are hiding, elections between hard-core Islamist parties and the moderate Awami National Party resulted in a rout by the ANP.

It is often said that elections do not a democracy make. That is certainly true. However, let us imagine for a moment what would have happened if, say, Hamas had been allowed to take its rightful place, albeit with certain restrictions and limitations, as the freely elected government in Palestine (a difficult exercise, to be sure, considering the bloody events that followed in the wake of its parliamentary victory over Fatah). Is it inconceivable that Hamas would have undergone a transformation similar to the one that occurred with the Muslim Brotherhood in Egypt, or, for that matter, with Fatah itself, which was designated a terrorist entity until it became an internationally recognized political entity (and ally to the United States and Israel)? Would, for example, the horror of Um al-Nasr have been blamed on the Hamas government instead of on Israel or the United States? In other words, had Hamas been given the opportunity to govern and fail, would it still enjoy the popular support it receives from Palestinians?

Or would the people have turned against it in favor of a less ideological, more accommodating, and more effective political party like Fatah, much as Fatah's failures turned the people toward Hamas? We may never know. Yet one thing is certain. While it is true that elections do not a democracy make, in a place like Palestine, two consecutive free and fair elections would have been a pretty good start.

In the end, there is really no choice in the matter. It is inconceivable that democratic reform could take place throughout the Middle East without the active participation of Islamist parties. Even more radical groups such as Hamas and Hizballah must be brought into the political fold. Despite their continued terrorist activities, these two remain the most dynamic political organizations in their countries. Simply labeling such organizations "nonstate entities" (as though there exists a cohesive Palestinian or Lebanese state) and thus dismissing their claims to political legitimacy will not diminish their power or their popularity. However, allowing these religious nationalists to participate more fully in the political process—albeit within certain accepted parameters—could conceivably force them to moderate their radical ideologies, as occurred with the Muslim Brotherhood and the AKP.

As we have seen, religious nationalism—whether Zionist, Christianist, or Islamist—is unavoidable in a globalized and increasingly borderless world. But that may not be such a bad thing. Between the extremes of secular authoritarianism and Jihadist fanaticism (often the only two options in this challenging and dangerous region), Islamism may be the preferable middle ground. It may in fact be the antidote to Jihadism.

Of course, there are those who, regardless of past performance or precedent, continue to insist that Islam and democracy are simply incompatible, that a party espousing Islamic values can never be democratic. Yet not only does such a view ignore the many successful Islamically influenced democratic movements—in Indonesia, Malaysia, Senegal, Morocco, Egypt, and Bangladesh—it makes the hope for political reform in the Muslim world a more distant prospect.

Nowhere has this fundamental truth been more definitively proven than in Gaza. For however one views the cycle of violence between Israel and the Palestinians (as a conflict over land and resources or as a cosmic war for the favor of God), whatever credence one gives to the idea that Islamist groups can evolve into responsible political parties, however one feels about the hope for peace in the Middle East, this one thing is clear: it was not the promise of democracy but the retraction of that promise that led to the fracturing of the Palestinians, the blockade of Gaza, the war between Hamas and Israel, and, ultimately, the devastation of 1.5 million Palestinian lives. Therefore, it will not be the rollback of democracy but rather its continued promotion that, in the long run, brings peace and stability, not just to Palestine but to the whole of the Middle East. It will also be the firm, patient, aggressive push for greater political participation by all parties in the region that ultimately defeats Global Jihadism, because it is precisely the absence of such participation, and the grievances that result, that fuels the movement's fires and keeps it alive. It is not enough, in other words, to merely seek out and destroy Jihadist militants. We must also strive to create an open religious and political environment in every Muslim majority state that will blunt the appeal of Jihadist ideologues. The War on Terror, as we have known it, may be over. But the struggle to counter Global Jihadism as a social movement has, in many ways, just begun.

## Acknowledgments

This book could not have been written without the support of the following people: Amanda Fortini, Ian Werrett, Mark Juergensmeyer, Richard Appelbaum, Lisa Hajjar, Derek Shearer, Nazanin Angoshtari, Megan Christopher, Will Murphy, Elyse Cheney, Courtney Turco, Nicole Steed, Howie Sanders, and so many others.

# Glossary

**Al-Nakba:** "The Catastrophe." The term Palestinians use to refer to the birth of the state of Israel and the refugee crisis that ensued as a result.

**Al-wala' wal-bara':** The doctrine of loyalty and enmity at the heart of the Jihadist movement.

**Caliph:** The political head of the Islamic community. The office of caliph was dismantled by Mustafa Kemal Atatürk in 1924.

**Christianism/Dominionism:** Christian religious nationalism; Christianity as a political ideology.

**Christian Zionism:** A movement of evangelical Protestant supporters of the state of Israel.

**Dar al-Islam:** "The land of Islam." Territory under the control of Islamic authorities.

**Dar al-kufr:** "The land of unbelief." Territory not under the control of Islamic authorities.

**Eretz Yisrael:** Greater Israel. The biblical Land of Israel.

**Evangelicalism:** A Protestant Christian social movement that began in eighteenth-century Britain.

**Fundamentalism:** Twentieth-century American evangelical movement.

**Global Jihadism:** A militant Sunni Muslim social movement with its roots in the Arab reform movements (Salafism) of the twentieth century.

**Gush Emunim:** "The Believers' Bloc." A movement of radical Jewish settlers in Israel.

**Hovevei Zion:** "Lovers of Zion." A Jewish settler movement founded by Leon Pinsker.

**Islamism:** Islamic religious nationalism; Islam as a political ideology.

**Islamofascism:** This word has no meaning.

**Jahaliyyah:** The Time of Ignorance. The period in the Arabian Peninsula prior to the rise of Islam.

*Kafir:* An apostate.

**Pan-Arabism:** A political ideology seeking the unification of the Arab world.

**Qutbist:** An adherent of the Egyptian intellectual and radical Muslim Brotherhood member Sayyid Qutb.

**Religious Zionism:** A movement of Israeli Jews who seek to reestablish biblical Israel.

**Salafism:** A twentieth-century Sunni Islamic movement that seeks a spiritual return to the early days of the Muslim community.

**Shahadah:** The Muslim profession of faith: "There is no god but God and Muhammad is God's Messenger."

**Shariah:** Islamic law.

*Takfir:* The practice of unilaterally declaring a Muslim to be an apostate.

**Temple Mount/Haram as-Sharif:** The platform atop Mount Moriah in Jerusalem where the Temple of Jerusalem once stood and where now stands the Dome of the Rock.

'*Ulama:* Islam's clerical class; the body of Islamic religious scholars.

*Ummah:* The worldwide community of Muslims.

**Wahhabism**: Ultraconservative sect of Islam founded in the nineteenth century by the Arabian reformer Muhammad ibn Abd al-Wahhab. Also called Muwahiddun.

**Waqf**: A religious endowment in Islam. Also refers to Jerusalem's Islamic religious authorities.

**Zealots**: A heterogeneous movement of Jewish radicals who led a rebellion against Rome in first-century Palestine.

**Zionism**: A secular nationalist movement in support of a Jewish state.

# Notes

## Introduction  Us Versus Them

3 "Purify your soul"
The complete text in English can be found on the *Guardian* website
(I have edited the original Arabic text for style and brevity):
www.guardian.co.uk/world/2001/sep/30/terrorism.september113.
Juan Cole argues that the text was "probably authored by Muhammad Atta himself, the only Egyptian on the hijacking team";
www.juancole.com/essays/qaeda.htm.

5 a *cosmic war*
The term "cosmic war" belongs to Mark Juergensmeyer, *Terror in
the Mind of God* (Berkeley: University of California Press, 2003).

6 "all appearances to the contrary"
Bruce Lincoln, *Holy Terrors: Thinking About Religion After September
11* (Chicago: University of Chicago Press, 2003), 17.

7 "establish the truth"
Quoted in Lawrence Wright, *The Looming Tower: Al-Qaeda and the
Road to 9/11* (New York: Knopf, 2006), 142.

8 **terrorism industry**

See John Mueller, *Overblown: How Politicians and the Terrorism Industry Inflate National Security Threats and Why We Believe Them* (New York: Free Press, 2006), and his excellent article "Is There Still a Terrorist Threat? The Myth of the Omnipresent Enemy," *Foreign Affairs*, September–October 2006.

8 **"to live in a state of war"**

Juergensmeyer, *Terror in the Mind of God*, 158.

8 **"In normal times"**

Eric Hoffer, *True Believer* (New York: Harper & Row, 1951), 163.

9 **"the focal point"**

Quoted in Gary Wills, "A Country Ruled by Faith," *The New York Review of Books*, November 16, 2006.

9 **"rid the world of evil"**

George W. Bush, speech at a multifaith prayer service, National Cathedral, Washington, D.C., September 14, 2001: "Our responsibility to history is already clear: to answer these attacks and rid the world of evil." See Charles Babington, "Bush: U.S. Must 'Rid the World of Evil,'" *The Washington Post*, September 14, 2001.

9 **"This is a transcendent evil"**

John McCain, interview with Jon Stewart, *The Daily Show with Jon Stewart*, May 19, 2008.

9 **"think[s] the opposite"**

See Anne E. Kornblut, "Bush Shifting Public Focus to Terrorism and Iraq War," *The New York Times*, August 31, 2006.

9 **"Our enemy is a spiritual enemy"**

From a speech given by Lieutenant General William G. Boykin at the Good Shepherd Church, Sandy, Oregon, June 21, 2003.

10 **that number now stands at nearly two thirds**

See David Barrett et al., *World Christian Encyclopedia: A Comparative Survey of Churches and Religions—AD 30 to 2200* (London: Oxford University Press, 2001).

11 **religious grievances are no less valid**

On this point, see Talal Asad, *On Suicide Bombing* (New York: Columbia University Press, 2007).

## CHAPTER ONE The Borderless Self

16 **"starve the Palestinian Authority"**
Steven Erlanger, "U.S. and Israelis Are Said to Talk of Hamas Ouster," *The New York Times*, February 14, 2006.

16 **"sewage tsunami"**
See "Flood of Sewage in Gaza Kills at Least 4," *The New York Times*, March 27, 2007.

18 **"a group of people united"**
Ernest Renan, "What Is a Nation?" (Qu'est-ce qu'une nation?), lecture given at the Sorbonne on March 11, 1882. The speech is published in Geoff Eley and Ronald Grigor Suny, eds., *Becoming National: A Reader* (New York: Oxford University Press, 1996), 41–55.

18 **in search of game and refuge**
See Nayan Chanda, *Bound Together: How Traders, Preachers, Adventurers, and Warriors Shaped Globalization* (New Haven, Conn.: Yale University Press, 2007).

19 **"The intensification of economic"**
Hans-Henrik Holm and Georg Sørensen, eds., *Whose World Order? Uneven Globalization and the End of the Cold War* (Boulder, Colo.: Westview Press, 1995), 1. See also Paul M. Lubeck, "The Islamic Revival," in *Global Social Movements*, ed. Robin Cohen and Shirin M. Rai (London: Athlone Press, 2000), 146–164.

19 **"a concept that refers"**
Roland Robertson, *Globalization: Social Theory and Global Culture* (London: Sage, 1992), 8.

19 **"a community of common descent"**
Anthony D. Smith, *National Identity* (Reno: University of Nevada Press, 1991), 3–15. See also his *The Nation in History* (Hanover, N.H.: University Press of New England, 2000); *Nationalism: Theory, Ideology, History* (Cambridge, England: Polity, 2001); and *Nations and Nationalism in a Global Era* (Cambridge, England: Polity, 1995).

20 **"imagined community"**
Benedict Anderson, *Imagined Communities: Reflections on the Origin and Spread of Nationalism* (London: Verso, 2006).

20 **who belongs and who does not**
See Peter Mandeville, *Transnational Muslim Politics* (London: Routledge, 2003).

21  "men are not tied to one another"
Edmund Burke, *The Works of the Right Honourable Edmund Burke,*
vol. 6 (London: Oxford University Press, 1907), 155.

21  the entity that claims a monopoly
See Max Weber, *Politics as a Vocation* (Minneapolis: Fortress Press,
1972). On the same topic, see Michel Foucault, *Discipline and Punish*
(New York: Vintage, 1995), and *The History of Sexuality,* vol. 1 (New
York: Vintage, 1990).

22  Witness the fragmentation of the former Yugoslavia
On this point, see Jerry Z. Miller, "Us and Them," *Foreign Affairs*
(March–April 2008).

24  In Arabic, *jihad* literally means "struggle"
The word "jihad" occurs thirty-five times in the Qur'an, but in only
four verses is it explicitly used to mean "war" (eleven uses are expressly pacifistic; the rest are open to multiple interpretations,
some contradictory), an indication of the tensions that existed in
the early Muslim community when it came to issues of war and violence. See Richard Bonney, *Jihad: From Qur'an to Bin Laden* (New
York: Palgrave, 2005), 28–29.

25  "wants to keep jihad alive"
Bin Laden, interview given to *Ummat* magazine, Karachi, September 28, 2001. Italics mine.

25  "the protector of all other deeds"
Maulana Masood Azhar, *The Virtues of Jihad* (Karachi: Mahle Sun-
nah Wal Jama'at Publications, 2001).

25  "Everyone not performing"
Sheikh Abdullah ibn Yusuf Azzam, *Join the Caravan* (London:
Azzam Publications, 2001).

26  "a symptom of the disease"
John Gray, *Al-Qaeda and What It Means to Be Modern* (New York:
New Press, 2003), 26.

26  "anyone who believes"
Quoted in Jarret M. Brachman, *Global Jihadism: Theory and Practice*
(London: Routledge, 2008), 31.

26  so as to make it strictly
See Faisal Devji, *Landscapes of the Jihad* (New York: Cornell University Press, 2005), 25.

27  Jarret Brachman
Brachman, *Global Jihadism*, 39–40.

28  "setting up the kingdom"
Sayyed Qutb, *Milestones* (Birmingham, England: Maktabah, 2006), 27.

28  "Those who consider themselves Muslim"
Quoted in I. M. Abu-Rabi, *Intellectual Origins of Islamic Resurgence in the Modern Arab World* (Albany: State University of New York Press, 1996), 130.

29  Abd al-Wahhab
I think Natana DeLong-Bas is right when she asserts in her brilliant biography of Abd al-Wahhab, *Wahhabi Islam* (Oxford: Oxford University Press, 2004), that he was introduced to ibn Taymiyyah through two prominent scholars: Sheikh Abd Allah ibn Ibrahim ibn Sayf from Najd and Shaykh Muhammad Hayat al-Hindi. DeLong-Bas questions whether Wahhab himself was as avid a follower of ibn Taymiyyah as he is often made out to be.

30  "religious nationalists"
See Fawaz Gerges, *The Far Enemy* (Cambridge, England: Cambridge University Press, 2005), 29; also *Journey of the Jihadist* (New York: Harcourt, 2007).

30  "The road to Jerusalem"
Quoted from the title of an article written by Zawahiri in the Jihadist newspaper *Al-Mujahidun*, April 26, 1995.

31  Islamism was doomed to fail
See Umar F. Abd-Allah, *The Islamic Struggle in Syria* (Berkeley, Calif.: Mizan Press, 1983).

31  "We realized we were a nation"
Quoted in Gerges, *The Far Enemy*, 63.

32  "The struggle to establish"
Ayman Zawahiri, *Knights under the Prophet's Banner*, serialized in *Al-Sharq al-Aswat*, December 2–10, 2001.

33  "resolves the mental complex"
Quoted in Brynjar Lia, *Architect of Global Jihad: The Life of Al-Qaida Strategist Abu Musab al-Suri* (New York: Columbia University Press, 2008), 158–159.

CHAPTER TWO   A Land Twice Promised

35   "Ten measures of beauty"
     Babylonian Talmud, Tractate Kiddushin 49:2.

37   "The Temple Mount is in our hands"
     Ariel Sharon, quoted in Suzanne Goldenberg, "Rioting as Sharon
     Visits Islam Holy Site," *The Guardian*, September 29, 2000.

40   The paper was a *bordereau*
     An English translation of the memo is available at www.hrc.utexas
     .edu/research/fa/digitized/forzinetti/1.html.

41   "I should have realized"
     Quoted in Adam Kirsch, "The Most Shameful of Stains," *New York
     Sun*, July 11, 2006.

42   "by definition excludes"
     E. J. Hobsbawm, *Nations and Nationalism Since 1780* (Cambridge,
     England: Cambridge University Press, 1990), 169.

42   "the negative pole"
     Michel Winock, *Nationalism, Anti-Semitism, and Fascism in France*
     (Stanford, Calif.: Stanford University Press, 1998), 137.

42   "is always effected"
     Ernest Renan, "What Is a Nation?" in *Nation and Narration*, ed.
     Homi K. Bhabha (London: Routledge, 1992), 8–22; 11.

43   "Auto-Emancipation"
     For the complete text, see Leon Pinsker, "Auto-Emancipation: An
     Appeal to His People by a Russian Jew," trans. from the German by
     Dr. D. S. Blondheim, in *Essential Texts of Zionism* (Jerusalem: Feder-
     ation of American Zionists, 1916).

45   "Palestine is our"
     Theodor Herzl, *The Jewish State: An Attempt at a Modern Solution of
     the Jewish Question,* trans. Jacob de Haas (New York: Federation of
     American Zionists, 1917), 12.

45   "The Bride is beautiful"
     Quoted in Avi Shlaim, *The Iron Wall* (New York: Norton,
     2001), 3.

45   "We must expropriate"
     Quoted in Benny Morris et al., eds., *The Birth of the Palestinian
     Refugee Problem, 1947–1949* (Cambridge, England: Cambridge Uni-
     versity Press, 2003), 41.

45  "the vast majority of Palestine's Arabs"
Benny Morris, "Revisiting the Palestine Exodus of 1948," in *The War for Palestine,* ed. Eugene L. Rogen and Avi Shlaim (Cambridge, England: Cambridge University Press, 2001), 37–59; 47.

45  "The Arabs will have to go"
Ben-Gurion's letter to his son is quoted in Ilan Pappe, *The Ethnic Cleansing of Palestine* (Oxford, England: Oneworld Publications, 2006), 23.

46  "superstition and fanaticism"
Quoted in Amy Dockser Marcus, *Jerusalem 1913* (New York: Viking, 2007), 37.

47  "With the evacuation"
Quoted in Morris, *The War for Palestine,* 42.

47  "It was not as though"
"Golda Meir Scorns Soviets," *The Washington Post,* June 16, 1969.

48  (Palestine's Christians, however)
See Charles D. Smith, *Palestine and the Arab-Israeli Conflict* (Boston: St. Martin's Press, 2001), 45.

49  made constructing a national identity
See Ghassan Kanafani, *The 1936–39 Revolt in Palestine* (New York: Committee for a Democratic Palestine, 1978), 26.

49  "an outpost of culture"
Quoted in Baylis Thomas, *How Israel Was Won* (Lanham, Md.: Lexington Books, 1999), 4.

49  "The four great powers"
Quoted in Christopher Sykes, *Crossroads to Israel* (Cleveland: World Publishing, 1965), 5.

50  "absurd, impracticable, and unjust"
Quoted in Shlaim, *The Iron Wall,* 27.

50  "as it fell short of the full-blown"
Ibid., 25.

50  "The partition of Palestine"
Ibid.

50  "I am certain we will be able to settle"
Ibid., 21.

51  Of the ten million Palestinians
A complete count of all Palestinian refugees and displaced persons is available at www.badil.org.

51  nearly half of the West Bank
    See Yehezkel Lein, *Land Grab: Israel's Settlement Policy in the West
    Bank* (Jerusalem: B'Tselem, May 2002), 93.

52  The wall has already devoured
    See Alternative Information Center, "The Separation Wall in East
    Jerusalem: Economic Consequences," available at www.alternative
    news.org/images/stories/downloads/socioeconomic_bulletin_
    11-12.pdf.

54  "They kill *us*"
    This anecdote is based on a conversation with a woman, who shall
    remain unnamed, who had been on the journey from Britain to
    Mecca and then to Israel with Mohammed Siddique Khan.

54  "injustice framing"
    William Gamson, "The Social Psychology of Collective Action,"
    *Frontiers in Social Movement Theory,* ed. Aldon D. Morris (New
    Haven, Conn.: Yale University Press, 1992), 53–76. This is an impor-
    tant term for our study of Jihadism because master frames built on
    repression resonate well with disparate groups, fostering a sense of
    alliance among competing organizations such as Hizballah, Hamas,
    and al-Qa'ida. See also Scott Hunt, Robert Benford, and David A.
    Snow, "Identity Fields: Framing Processes and the Social Construc-
    tion of Movement Identities," *New Social Movements,* ed. Enrique
    Larana (Philadelphia: Temple University Press, 1994), 185–208.

54  Successful framing has the power
    Steven M. Buechler, *Social Movements in Advanced Capitalism* (New
    York: Oxford University Press, 2000), 41.

55  transition from collective identity
    Ibid.

55  into simple, black-and-white ones
    On the role of political violence and the state, see Donatella della
    Porta, *Social Movements, Political Violence, and the State* (Cambridge,
    England: Cambridge University Press, 1995). See also Sidney G.
    Tarrow, *Power in Movement* (Cambridge, England: Cambridge Uni-
    versity Press, 1998), 94.

56  "You have destroyed nature"
    Bin Laden, quoted in Bruce Lawrence, ed., *Messages to the World:
    The Statements of Osama bin Laden* (London: Verso, 2005), 168.

56  "favor the rich"
    Bin Laden, quoted in *The Al-Qaeda Reader,* xxx.

56  widely acknowledged election fraud
    See *The Al-Qaeda Reader,* 217.

CHAPTER THREE  Zeal for Your House Consumes Me

61  "came to him as naturally as"
    James Carroll, *Crusade: Chronicles of an Unjust War* (New York: Metropolitan Books, 2004), 7. See also his essay "The Bush Crusade," *The Nation,* September 20, 2004.

62  "The enemy of America"
    George W. Bush, Address to Joint Session of Congress, September 20, 2001. For the complete text, see www.whitehouse.gov/news/releases/2001/09/20010920-8.html.

63  "Our goal is for our Muslim community"
    Bin Laden, quoted in *Messages to the World,* 135.

63  "The odd thing about this"
    Bin Laden, quoted in ibid., 121.

63  The Crusades have long
    Depending on how you count, there were four, five, or six Crusades. Along with Christopher Tyerman, I count five Crusades: the First Crusade (1095–1099) involved the recapture of Jerusalem; the Second Crusade (1145–1149) led to the conquering of Syrio-Palestinian ports and Christian frontiers in Spain; the Third Crusade (1188–1192) resulted in the loss of Jerusalem to Saladin; the Fourth Crusade (1198–1204) and Fifth Crusade (1213–1229) pretty much institutionalized crusading as a means of Christian revivalism. See Christopher Tyerman, *Fighting for Christendom: Holy War and the Crusades* (London: Oxford University Press, 2004).

63  "The Crusader spirit"
    Quoted in ibid., 204.

64  "This battle is not between"
    Bin Laden, quoted in *The Al-Qaeda Reader,* 261.

64  a single *corpus christianum*
    See Ronald H. Bainton, *Christian Attitudes Toward War and Peace* (New York: Abingdon Press, 1960), 116.

64  **"Bush said, 'Either you are' "**
Bin Laden, quoted in *Messages to the World*, 121–122.

64  **"the practical business"**
Tyerman, *Fighting for Christendom*, 142–143.

65  **"I, or rather the Lord"**
There are at least four versions of Pope Urban's speech. This one is from the chronicles of Fulcher of Chartres, quoted in *A Source Book for Medieval History*, ed. Oliver J. Thatcher and Edgar Holmes McNeal (New York: Scribner's, 1905), 513–517.

66  **"This day"**
The Chronicles of Raymond of Agiles can be found in Bainton, *Christian Attitudes toward War and Peace*, 112–113.

66  **The concept of cosmic war**
For an outline of divine war ideas in the Ancient Near East, see Sa-Moon Kang, *Divine War in the Old Testament and in the Ancient Near East* (Berlin, 1989); Moshe Weinfeld, "Divine Intervention in War in Ancient Israel and in the Ancient Near East," *History, Historiography, and Interpretation: Studies in Biblical and Cuneiform Literatures*, ed. H. Tadmor and M. Weinfeld (Leiden, 1987); and Michael G. Hasel, *Military Practice and Polemic: Israel's Laws of Warfare in Near Eastern Perspective* (Berrien Springs, Mich.: Andrews University Press, 2005).

67  **Israelites and their god**
The god of Israel is called both El and Yahweh throughout the Hebrew Bible. Although in Judaism these two gods would eventually merge into one, it is vital to recognize El and Yahweh as two very different deities with distinct and separate histories, mythologies, rituals, and cults. El was the High God of ancient Canaan, who made a covenant with Abraham. Yahweh was likely a local Egyptian deity named after a seminomadic, militant tribe that resided somewhere near the Sinai, where Moses first encountered him in the form of a burning bush. See Johannes C. De Moor, *The Rise of Yahwism* (Leuven, 1990). Throughout this book I will refer to both deities simply as God. The image of God as warrior can be found in the oldest hymns of the Bible, such as the Song of Deborah (Judg. 5:1–31) and the Song of the Sea (Exod. 15:1–21). For God as a man of war, see Millard C. Lind, *Yahweh Is a Warrior: The Theology of Warfare in Ancient Israel* (Scottsdale, Pa.: Herald Press, 1980);

Patrick Miller, *The Divine Warrior in Early Israel* (Cambridge, Mass., 1973) and "God the Warrior: A Problem in Biblical Interpretation and Apologetics," *Interpretation* 19 (1965): 39–46; and Mark S. Smith, *The Early History of God: Yahweh and the Other Deities in Ancient Israel* (San Francisco: Harper & Row, 1990).

**68  the excitation of nature**
See Weinfeld, "Divine Intervention," 124.

**68  God is actively present**
God's presence can also be reflected either through emblems or standards (such as the Ark of the Covenant) or through the consecration of weapons, which essentially transforms them into instruments of the divine. For more examples of God's presence in battle see Exod. 23:29–30, 34:11; Deut. 7:23; Josh. 2:24, 6:2, 6:16, 8:1, 10:8, 10:10, 24:7; Judg. 3:28, 4:7, 4:15, 6:3, 7:9, 7:22, 18:10, 20:28; 1 Sam. 5:11, 7:10, 13:3, 14:12, 17:46, 23:4, 24:4, 26:8; 1 Kings 20:28.

**68  (*herem,* in Hebrew)**
*Herem* is defined by the *Encyclopaedia Judaica* as "that which is separated from common use or contact either because it is proscribed as an abomination to God or because it is consecrated to God." As an adjective, *herem* is philologically linked to the Arabic word *haruma* ("forbidden" or "sacred"), from which the Qur'an derives the term for sanctuary: *haram.* However, the difference between the Hebrew *herem* and the Arabic *haram* (or, for that matter, between *herem* and the Hebrew word of sanctuary, *qodesh*) is that *herem* refers to a sanctified thing that has become wholly inaccessible and irredeemable to human beings and must therefore be set apart for destruction. See Philip D. Stern, *The Biblical Herem: A Window on Israel's Religious Experience* (Atlanta: Scholars Press, 1992), and M. Greenberg, "Herem," in *Encyclopaedia Judaica,* ed. Cecil Roth et al. (New York, 1971–72), 344–351. *Herem* need not be understood solely as a synonym for destruction. There are numerous usages of the word that have nothing to do with war (Exod. 22:19; Lev. 27:28–29). See R. D. Nelson, "Herem and the Deuteronomic Social Conscience," *Deuteronomy and the Deuteronomic Literature,* ed. M. Vervenne and J. Lust (Leuven, 1997), 39–54.

**69  "ethnic cleansing as a means"**
John Collins, "The Zeal of Phinehas: The Bible and the Legitimation of Violence," *Journal of Biblical Literature* 122, no. 1 (2003), 7.

**69   the principal means**

This point is made brilliantly by the great Julius Wellhausen in his
*Prolegomena to the History of Ancient Israel* (New York: Meridian
Books, 1957).

**70   The Zealots were not**

For more on the Zealots, see Martin Hengel, *The Zealots* (Edin-
burgh: T&T Clark, 1989); H. Paul Kingdon, "The Origins of the
Zealots," *New Testament Studies* 19 (1968), 74–81; Morton Smith,
"Zealots and Sicarii: Their Origins and Relation," *Harvard Theological Review* 64 (1971): 1–19; David Rhodes, *Israel in Revolution: 6–74
C.E.* (Philadelphia: Fortress, 1976). Morton Smith has proven that
the term "zealot" did not reflect an organized political faction during the lifetime of Judas the Galilean. For more on sectarianism in
first-century Judaism, see Jeff S. Anderson, *The Internal Diversifica-
tion of Second Temple Judaism* (Lanham, Md.: University Press of
America, 2002).

**72   first-century historian Flavius Josephus**

See Flavius Josephus, *The Jewish War*, trans. G. A. Williamson
(New York: Dorset Press, 1985). That Judas the Galilean was likely
a rabbi learned in the Torah is suggested by Josephus's numerous
descriptions of him as a *sophist*, a word that in Greek means
"learned man" or "teacher" but also connotes some measure of
connivance. Josephus merely refers to this group as a fourth
philosophy (along with the Sadducees, Pharisees, and Essenes),
rather than formally naming them as such. However, in order to
reflect the fact that Judas's zealots may not have been the same
zealots who would form a distinct party and rebel against Rome,
we shall continue to refer to them hereafter as the Fourth Philosophy.

**76   The last of the rebels**

Josephus claims that the story of Masada came to him via two
women and five children who survived the massacre by hiding in
the aqueducts beneath Herod's palace.

## CHAPTER FOUR  An Army of Believers

**80  the core belief of Religious Zionism**

Religious Zionism has its roots in the teachings of Rabbi Yehuda hai Alkalai (1798–1878).

**80  "an external shell"**

See Motti Inbari, "Religious Zionism and the Temple Mount Dilemma—Key Trends," *Israel Studies* 12, no. 2 (2007): 29–47.

**81  "Our faith is firm"**

Quoted in Shlomo Zalman Shragai, "Rabbi Avraham Hacohen Kook on the Restitution of the Place of Our Temple to the People of Israel," *Sinai* 85 (1978): 193–198; 197.

**81  A story is told about Rabbi Goren**

See Gershom Gorenberg, *The End of Days: Fundamentalism and the Struggle for the Temple Mount* (New York: Simon and Schuster, 2001), 100.

**81  Gush Emunim**

Although the Gush arose from the victory of 1967, it wasn't until 1974 that it became an official organization.

**81  "a cruel divine operation"**

Quoted in Gershom Gorenberg, *The Accidental Empire: Israel and the Birth of the Settlements, 1967–1977* (New York: Times Books, 2006), 91; also 90–92, 303.

**81  Settlement was never meant**

"The national-unity government headed by Levi Eshkol was established shortly before the outbreak of war in June 1967. During the months immediately following the war, this government did not have any clear policy regarding Israeli settlement in the West Bank. The initial inclination of most of the members of the government was to hold the territory as a bargaining chip for future negotiations." Yehezkel Lein, *Land Grab: Israel's Settlement Policy in the West Bank* (Jerusalem: B'Tselem, 2002), 6–7.

**81  "The wholeness of the Land"**

Quoted in Gorenberg, *Accidental Empire*, 92.

**82  "a semi-official governing body"**

Ian Lustick, *For the Land and the Lord: Jewish Fundamentalism in Israel* (New York: Council on Foreign Relations, 1988), 8.

82  "re-Judaization movement"
    See Gilles Kepel, *The Revenge of God: The Resurgence of Islam, Christianity and Judaism in the Modern World* (University Park: Pennsylvania State University Press, 1994).

83  "whether they are on"
    Isabel Kershner, "Radical Settlers Take On Israel," *The New York Times,* September 26, 2008.

84  "According to the Halacha"
    www.cnn.com/WORLD/9511/rabin/amir/11-06/index.html.

84  sacrificing himself
    "Rabin Assassin's Wife: Yigal Amir Sacrificed Himself for His People," *Haaretz,* available at www.haaretz.com/hasen/spages/915701.html.

84  A 2006 poll conducted by the Dahaf Institute
    See http://www.ynetnews.com/articles/0,7340,L-3320266,00.html.

84  a packed soccer stadium in Haifa
    See http://www.ynet.co.il/english/articles/0,7340,L-3467773,00.html.

84  "This is God's land"
    Pat Robertson, quoted in Stephen Sizer, *Christian Zionism: Road Map to Armageddon?* (Leicester, Mass.: Inter-Varsity Press, 2004), 251.

84  so-called Christian Zionists
    Christian Zionism, as the movement of evangelical supporters of Israel is called, actually predates the Six-Day War, predates even the birth of the state of Israel. Christian Zionist organizations include the Christian Friends of Israel, the Christian Israel Public Affairs Committee, Voices United for Israel, Christians United for Israel, and International Christian Embassy in Jerusalem, to name just a few.

85  "an international plot"
    Mike Evans, *Jerusalem Betrayed* (Nashville: Thomas Nelson, 1997), 167.

85  "God doesn't care"
    Hagee, quoted in Sizer, *Christian Zionism,* 233.

85  "The line between"
    Yaakov Lappin, "Christians: We'll Fight for Israel," www.YNETnews.com, September 27, 2006.

85  "seeks not only to destroy"
    Lindsey, quoted in Sizer, *Christian Zionism,* 248.

86  "We Americans are"
Quoted in Walter Russell Mead, "The New Israel and the Old,"
*Foreign Affairs,* July–August 2008, 28–46; 35.

86  "America has received"
Jonathan Edwards, quoted in Conrad Cherry, *God's New Israel*
(Upper Saddle River, N.J.: Prentice Hall, 1971), 57.

86  "Rebellion to tyrants"
There is an excellent sketch of that first seal here:
www.greatseal.com/committees/firstcomm/reverse.html.

87  "America," preached the
Cherry, *God's New Israel,* 15.

87  "now and forever the palladium"
Quoted in Cherry, *God's New Israel,* 225.

87  "by the saints against"
Ibid., 272.

87  "were the very creatures of Satan"
Ibid.

88  "The world is too small"
Ibid., 276.

88  "The Christian home"
Quoted in Jeff Sharlett, "Soldiers of Christ," *Harper's,* May 2005.
Ted Haggard capped off decades of preaching against drugs and
homosexuality by admitting in 2007 to repeatedly having bought
methamphetamines and sexual services from his gay prostitute.

89  "The local church"
Quoted in Frances FitzGerald, "A Disciplined Charging Army,"
*The New Yorker,* May 18, 1981.

89  evangelicals are far more likely
See George Marsden's classic text on the subject, *Fundamentalism
and American Culture* (New York: Oxford University Press, 2006), 9.

89  A survey of the twenty-four
James K. Wellman, Jr., "Is War Normal for American Evangelical
Religion?" in *Belief and Bloodshed: Religion and Violence Across Time
and Tradition,* ed. Wellman (Lanham, Md.: Rowman and Littlefield,
2007), 195–210. See *American Piety in the 21st Century: New Insights to
the Depth and Complexity of Religion in the US, Selected Findings from
the Baylor Religion Survey,* September 2006.

**90** **a coalition of diverse**
See George M. Marsden, *Understanding Fundamentalism and Evangelicalism* (Grand Rapids, Mich.: Eerdmans, 1991); see also Timothy L. Smith, "The Evangelical Kaleidoscope and the Call to Christian Unity," *Christian Scholar's Review* 15, no. 2 (1986): 125–140.

**91** **"A Fundamentalist is"**
Marsden, *Understanding Fundamentalism*, 1.

**92** **more than a third of all Americans**
For the results of the Gallup and Princeton polls, see www.wheaton .edu/isae/Gallup-Bar-graph.html.

**93** **"the universe is divided"**
Marsden, *Understanding Fundamentalism*, 117.

**93** **"born again"**
Although the term "born again" comes from the New Testament ("I say to you, unless one is born again, he cannot see the kingdom of God"; John 3:3), the notion that salvation belongs only to those who have been born again—that is, those with an individual relationship with Jesus—is rooted in the evangelical movement of the eighteenth and nineteenth centuries.

**93** **crisis, conflict, and threat**
On this point, see Christian Smith, *American Evangelicalism: Embattled and Thriving* (Chicago: University of Chicago Press, 1999), 89; 120–153.

**93** **one thousand evangelical megachurches**
See Luisa Kroll, "Megachurches, Megabusiness," *Forbes*, September 12, 2003.

**93** **approval rating of 80 to 100 percent**
See Chris Hedges, *American Fascists* (New York: Free Press, 2006), 22–23.

**94** **"lose its identity and purpose"**
Smith, *American Evangelicalism*, 120–121.

**94** **"Christianization" and "Americanization"**
On this point, see Joel A. Carpenter and W. R. Shenk, *Earthen Vessels: American Evangelicals and Foreign Missions, 1880–1980* (Grand Rapids, Mich.: Eerdmans, 1990).

**94** **"Dominionists" or "Christianists"**
For more on this movement, see Michelle Goldberg, *Kingdom Coming* (New York: Norton, 2007), and Hedges, *American Fascists*.

94   "redefine traditional democratic"
     Hedges, *American Fascists*, 8.

94   large numbers of American evangelicals
     See *Selected Findings from the Baylor Religion Survey*, September 2006,
     cited above.

95   "a dress rehearsal for Armageddon"
     http://jerusalemprayerteam.org/articles/nosurprise.asp.

95   "America is the hope"
     See Jim Wallis, "Dangerous Religion: George W. Bush's Theology
     of Empire," *Sojourner's*, September–October 2003.

95   "In this paradigm"
     Quoted in Kara Hopkins, "The Gospel According to Gerson,"
     *American Conservative*, November 19, 2007.

96   *military missionaries*
     www.severnsvalley.org/ministries/faithevangelism.asp.

96   "a quasi-federal entity"
     Quoted in a *Washington Post* editorial, "Pulling Rank on Religion,"
     August 13, 2007.

97   "government-paid missionaries"
     For full text and video, see www.militaryreligiousfreedom.org/
     press-releases/ccc_usafa.html.

97   an independent investigation
     "Report of Americans United for Separation of Church and State
     on Religious Coercion and Endorsement of Religion at the United
     States Air Force Academy"; available at www.au.org.

97   "burn in the fires of hell"
     See also Pam Zubeck, "Air Force Deems Chaplain's Call Appropri-
     ate," Colorado Springs *Gazette*, April 27, 2005.

97   eighteen full-time chaplains
     David Antoon, "The Cancer from Within," November 7, 2007;
     available at www.truthdig.org.

98   "Deployment and possibly deadly"
     www.cadence.org/home/who-we-are/a-strategic-ministry.

98   An investigation by the McClatchy Newspapers
     Jason Leopold, "U.S. Soldiers Launch Campaign to Convert Iraqis
     to Christianity," McClatchy Newspapers, May 28, 2008.

98   U.S. marines were caught
     Jamal Naji and Leila Fadel, "Iraqis Claim Marines Are Pushing

Christianity in Fallujah," McClatchy Washington Bureau, May 29, 2008.

99   **God instructed him**
     Arnon Regular, " 'Road Map Is a Life Saver for Us,' PM Abbas Tells *Hamas," Ha'aretz*, June 25, 2003.

99   **"Crusades-like messaging"**
     Robert Draper, "And He Shall Be Judged," *GQ*, March 24, 2009.

99   **battle between America and "radical Islam"**
     Neela Banerjee, "Religion and Its Role Are in Dispute at the Service Academies," *The New York Times*, June 25, 2008.

99   **"hunt down" the country's Muslim population**
     See http://english.aljazeera.net/news/asia/2009/05/200953201315854832.html.

99   **"a Christian crusader tasked with eliminating Muslims"**
     Jeremy Scahill, "Blackwater Founder Implicated in Murder," *The Nation*, August 4, 2009.

100  **"To my brother holy warriors"**
     Bin Laden, quoted in *Messages to the World*, 188.


CHAPTER FIVE  The Near and the Far

102  **"patent polytheism"**
     The full text of Zarqawi's letter is available at www.globalsecurity.org/wmd/library/news/iraq/2004/02/040212-al-zarqawi.htm.

104  **blowing himself up**
     Paul von Zielbauer, "U.S. Investigating Strike That Killed 15 Civilians," *The New York Times*, October 13, 2007; Christian Berthelsen, "Attack Kills 4 in Iraq on Holiday," *Los Angeles Times*, October 13, 2007.

104  **"there is little connection"**
     Robert Pape, *Dying to Win* (New York: Random House, 2005), 205.

104  **"We have no planes"**
     Quoted in Bruce Hoffman, *Inside Terrorism* (New York: Columbia University Press, 1998), 99.

105  **"Whoever purposely throws"**
     Hadith: Bukhari 7:670, narrated Abu Huraira.

105  **"the one issue on which"**
     Bin Laden, quoted in *Messages to the World*, 147.

106 "There is no neutrality"

Quoted in Wright, *The Looming Tower,* 190.

106 *"Wala'* inspires intimacy"

Muhammad Saeed al-Qahtani, *Al-Wala' wal-Bara' According to the Aqeedah of the Salaf;* available in English at http://islamworld.net/docs/wala.html.

106 "The difference between"

Maulana Masood Azhar, *Virtues of the Jihad* (Karachi: Idara Al-Khair, 2001).

106 "the very foundation of the religion"

Abu Muhammad 'Asim Al-Maqdisi, *Millat Ibrāhīm* [The Religion of Ibrāhīm] *and the Calling of the Prophets and Messengers and the Methods of the Transgressing Rulers in Dissolving It and Turning the Callers Away from It;* available in English on www.maktabah.net.

107 "If you were sincere"

Abu Hamza al-Masri's *Beware of Takfir* is available in English at www.scribd.com/doc/2402521/Beware-of-Takfir-Abu-Hamza-AIMISRI.

107 "Whoever loves an infidel"

For Zawahiri's complete text of "Al-Wala' wal-Bara' " in English, see *The Al-Qaeda Reader,* 84. Raymond Ibrahim translates this sentence as "Whoever does love an infidel is not a Believer."

107 "to reaffirm that"

The full text of the fatwa is available in English at http://amman message.com/index.php?option=com_content&task=view&id=33&Itemid=34.

108 allow him to challenge

See Abd al-Hakim ibn al-Matroudi, *The Hanbali School of Law and Ibn Taymiyya* (London: Routledge, 2006).

111 "unbelievers [and] hypocrites"

Ibn Taymiyyah's fatwa is recorded in full in Richard Bonney, *Jihad: From Qur'an to Bin Laden* (New York: Palgrave, 2005), 424–425.

111 "Jihad is valid"

Quoted in W. Montgomery Watt, *The Formative Period of Islamic Thought* (Oxford, England: Oneworld Publications, 1998), 292.

112 "To fight the Mongols"

Quoted in Johannes J. G. Jansen, *The Neglected Duty* (New York: Macmillan, 1986), 177.

113  "Jihad implies all kinds"
     Shaykh ul-Islaam Taqi-ud-Deen Ahmad ibn Taymiyyah, *The Religious and Moral Doctrine of Jihad*. The full text of this book is available in English at http://hss.fullerton.edu/comparative/Jihad_relmora.pdf.

114  "The rulers of this age"
     Translated in Jansen, *The Neglected Duty*, 169.

115  "If we look at the sources"
     Sayyid Qutb, *Milestones* (India: Islamic Book Service, 2006), 26–27.

115  "To fight an enemy"
     Jansen, *The Neglected Duty*, 192.

116  "The prayer ceremonies"
     Quoted in ibid., 55.

116  "God himself will"
     Ibid., 15–16.

117  "astonished and shaken"
     Wright, *The Looming Tower*, 50.

119  "Jihad is an obligation"
     Abdullah Azzam, *Defense of Muslim Lands*. The full text in English is available at www.islamistwatch.org/texts/azzam/defense/defense.html.

120  "advised Zawahiri to stop"
     Montasser al-Zayyat, *The Road to Al-Qaeda: The Story of Bin Laden's Right-Hand Man* (London: Pluto Press, 2004), 68–70.

121  "To kill the Americans"
     The text of the fatwa is available in *Messages to the World*, 58–62.

121  "to awaken the Islamic Nation"
     From al-Suri, *Global Islamic Resistance Call*, quoted in Brynjar Lia, *Architect of Global Jihad* (New York: Columbia University Press, 2008), 314–315.

122  terrorism must have
     See Jerrold M. Post, "Terrorist Psycho-logic: Terrorist Behavior as a Product of Psychological Forces," in *Origins of Terrorism*, ed. Walter Reich (Washington, D.C.: Woodrow Wilson Press, 1990), 25–40.

122  "to show the world"
     Lincoln, *Holy Terrors*, 17.

122  "a creed of great purity"
     Lawrence, *Messages to the World*, xxii.

122  "two separate camps"
Bin Laden, quoted in *The Al-Qaeda Reader*, 194.

122  "Jihad in the path"
Ayman Zawahiri, quoted in *The Al-Qaeda Reader*, 182.

123  "Excuse me Mr. Zawahiri"
Quoted in Peter Bergen, "The Unraveling," *The New Republic*, June 11, 2008.

123  "Zawahiri and bin Laden"
Ibid.

124  "a mode of activism"
See Jason Burke, *Al-Qaeda: Casting a Shadow of Terror* (London: I. B. Tauris, 2003), 8.

124  "It is not a group"
Quoted in Lawrence Wright, "The Master Plan," *The New Yorker*, September 11, 2006.

## CHAPTER SIX  Generation E

130  the state still maintains
Krishan Kumar makes this point rather nicely in "The Nation-State, The European Union, and Transnational Identities," in *Muslim Europe or Euro-Islam*, ed. Nezar AlSayyad and Manuel Castells (Lanham, Md.: Lexington Books, 2002), 53–68.

131  "consider themselves not"
T. R. Reid, *The United States of Europe* (New York: Penguin, 2004), 3.

133  "national cohesion"
Olivier Roy, *Secularism Confronts Islam* (New York: Columbia University Press, 2008), 30.

133  "symbols of a parallel world"
Mark Lander, "In Munich, Provocation in a Symbol of Foreign Faith," *The New York Times*, December 8, 2006.

133  less than 3 percent of Muslim women
"Uncomfortable Politics of Identity," *The Economist*, October 14, 2006, 68; Jane Perlez, "Muslims' Veils Test Limits of Britain's Tolerance," *The New York Times*, June 22, 2007; "Deconstructing the Veil," *The Economist*, October 14, 2006, 63.

134  "Not those owned by Chinese"
The quotation is taken from Chris Allen, "From Race to Religion:

The New Face of Discrimination," *Muslim Britain: Communities under Pressure,* ed. Tahir Abbas (London: Zed, 2005), 49–65; 55. See also Matthew Taylor, "BNP Accused of Exploiting Cartoons Row with Muslim Leaflet," *The Guardian,* October 5, 2006.

134  **that number had risen**
"Who Are the British National Party and What Do They Stand For?," Socialist Worker Online, May 24, 2008. The paper has a picture of the BNP founder, John Tyndall, in full Nazi regalia, posing in front of a photo of Adolf Hitler. "BNP Doubles Number of Councilors," http://news.bbc.co.uk/2/hi/uk_news/politics/4974870.stm, May 5, 2006; Dominic Casciani, "BNP Gains from Labour Disaffection," http://news.bbc.co.uk/1/hi/uk_politics/7382831.stm, May 4, 2008.

136  **by no means a modern**
The British historian E. J. Hobsbawm considers "primitive or archaic forms of social agitation," such as slave revolts and peasant uprisings, to be premodern forms of social movements. E. J. Hobsbawm, *Primitive Rebels* (New York: Norton, 1959), 1.

137  **to a world of self-identification**
See Steven M. Buechler, *Social Movements in Advanced Capitalism* (New York: Oxford University Press, 2000), 188.

137  **The French Revolution**
See Immanuel Wallerstein, "Antisystemic Movements: History and Dilemmas," in *Transforming the Revolution,* ed. Samir Amin et al. (New York: Monthly Review Press, 1990), 13–53. According to Wallerstein, the French Revolution formed the "ideological motifs of the modern world," which can be found in nearly all social movements that have followed, including Jihadism.

137  **a herd of cattle**
See Emile Durkheim, *Suicide: A Study in Sociology* (Glencoe, Ill.: Free Press, 1951).

138  **participants in social movements**
Michael Schwartz, *Radical Protest and Social Structure* (New York: Academic Press, 1976), 135.

138  **"normal, rational, institutionally rooted"**
Quoted in Buechler, *Social Movements in Advanced Capitalism,* 35.

138  **secularization theories**
Christian Smith, *Disruptive Religion* (New York: Routledge, 1996), 4.

139  A huge part of the success
Aldon Morris, "The Black Church in the Civil Rights Movement:
The SCLC as the Decentralized, Radical Arm of the Black
Church," in Smith, *Disruptive Religion*, 29–46.

139  "selective incentives"
See Mancur Olson, *The Logic of Collective Action* (Cambridge, Mass.:
Harvard University Press, 1965).

139  an automatic sense of authority
See Smith, *Disruptive Religion*, 9–22.

139  "internal enemy"
Quoted in Sharon Erickson Nepstad, "Popular Religion, Protest,
and Revolt: The Emergence of Political Insurgency in the
Nicaraguan and Salvadoran Churches of the 1960s–80s," in Smith,
*Disruptive Religion*, 105–124; 116.

140  "No official scholar's"
Bin Laden, quoted in *Messages to the World,* 141.

140  "tantamount to worshiping"
Ibid., 228.

140  "weld supporters together"
Sidney Tarrow, *Power in Movement* (Cambridge, England:
Cambridge University Press, 1998), 94. Tarrow views terrorism as
merely political violence in its most extreme, ritualized form.

141  familiar Christian symbols
See Nepstad, "Popular Religion, Protest, and Revolt."

142  "[Christ] says we must"
Phillip Berryman, *The Religious Roots of Rebellion* (New York: Orbis,
1984), 314.

142  "We know," Romero wrote
Ibid., 314–315.

143  "Either you are with the slaughtered"
Mark Juergensmeyer, *Global Rebellion* (Berkeley: University of California Press, 2008), 216.

143  "actions that begin"
Tarrow, *Power in Movement*, 94.

144  more than twenty million Muslims
Konrad Pedziwiatr, "Muslims in Europe: Demography and Organizations," in *Islam in the European Union,* ed. Yunas Samad and Katsuri Sen (Oxford, England: Oxford University Press, 2007), 26–59.

144   **Islam became a means**
      Robert J. Pauly, *Islam in Europe: Integration or Marginalization?*
      (Burlington, Vt.: Ashgate, 2004), 99.

145   **"the threat of the radical Islamists"**
      "Against Anti-Europeanism," *The Economist*, April 28, 2007, 40.

145   **84 percent of those**
      Marc Sageman, *Leaderless Jihad* (Philadelphia: University of Penn-
      sylvania Press, 2008), 65.

146   **"Euro-Islam"**
      See Bassam Tibi, "Muslim Migrants in Europe: Between Euro-
      Islam and Ghettoization," in *Muslim Europe or Euro-Islam*, ed. Nezar
      AlSayyad and Manuel Castells (Lanham, Md.: Lexington Books,
      2002), 31–52.

147   **"Extremism is an exaggerated"**
      Tarrow, *Power in Movement*, 4.

147   **only about 13 percent**
      Sageman, *Leaderless Jihad*, 52.

147   **since 2002, the German police**
      From an unpublished report prepared for Humanity in Action by
      Ben Harburg and Siddik Bakir, "'Die Geister, die ich rief!' (The
      Ghosts That I Awoke): German Anti-Terror Law and Religious Ex-
      tremism."

149   **"Don't you dare associate"**
      Bin Laden, quoted in *The Al-Qaeda Reader*, 252.

149   **"vernacular" forms of Islam**
      Jocelyn Cesari, "The Hybrid and Globalized Islam of Western Eu-
      rope," in *Islam in the European Union*, ed. Yunas Samad and Katsuri
      Sen (Oxford, England: Oxford University Press, 2007), 108–122; 113.

149   **"We find that the only"**
      Bin Laden, quoted in *The Al-Qaeda Reader*, 269.

149   **"I instruct the young people"**
      Ibid., 268.

150   **spoiling the emotional immediacy**
      See Olivier Roy, *Globalized Islam* (New York: Columbia University
      Press, 2004), 31.

151   **"When I went to Pakistan"**
      Hassan Butt, quoted in "My Brother the Bomber," *Prospect Maga-
      zine*, June 2007.

156 "We are decent people"
Ian Herbert, "How British Muslim Whose Partner Died in
7 July Attacks Confronted Bomber's Father," *The Independent*,
July 6, 2006.

156 in order to sufficiently assimilate
Roy, *Globalized Islam*, x.


CHAPTER SEVEN  The Middle Ground

163 "The fault lines"
Samuel Huntington, "The Clash of Civilizations?" *Foreign Affairs*
(Summer 1993).

163 "[It is] proven in the Qur'an"
Bin Laden, quoted in *Messages to the World*, 124.

164 "The underlying problem"
Samuel Huntington, *The Clash of Civilizations and the Remaking of
World Order* (New York: Simon and Schuster, 1996), 217.

165 nearly 80 percent of Muslims
Poll available at WorldPublicOpinion.org. It is not only Muslim-
majority states that hold unfavorable views of the United States:
77 percent of Spaniards, 63 percent of Germans, 44 percent of
Britons, and 61 percent of French people have negative perceptions
of the United States—all record highs.

165 "For sixty years"
Full text of speech available at www.state.gov/secretary/rm/2005/
48328.htm.

166 "to seek and support the growth"
Full text of speech available at www.whitehouse.gov/news/
releases/2005/01/20050120-1.html.

166 "All who live in tyranny"
Ibid.

167 "power in the world's least"
"Regression Analysis," *The Economist*, March 17, 2007, 52.

167 Large majorities throughout
See series of polls on Muslim perceptions of democracy available at
WorldPublicOpinion.org.

167 Gallup International
www.voice-of-the-people.net.

167   A Pew poll found
      http://pewglobal.org/reports/display.php?ReportID=253.

168   the country's first legitimate opposition party
      See James Traub, "Muslim Democrats?" *The New York Times Maga-*
      *zine*, April 29, 2007, 44–49.

169   "didn't bring up difficult issues"
      Rick Kelly, "Mubarak Regime Cracks Down on Opposition," World
      Socialist website, March 11, 2006; www.wsws.org/articles/2006/
      mar2006/egyp-m11.shtml.

170   "Anyone who calls for Islam"
      Ayman Zawahiri, quoted in *The Al-Qaeda Reader*, 136.

170   "Either you are with us"
      George W. Bush, address to Joint Session of Congress, September
      20, 2001. For the complete text, see www.whitehouse.gov/news/
      releases/2001/09/20010920-8.html.

171   "in this conflict"
      George W. Bush, address to the nation, October 7, 2001. For the
      complete text, see www.whitehouse.gov/news/releases/2001/10/
      20011007-8.html.

171   "My job is to communicate"
      Obama interview with Al-Arabiya television, January 26, 2009.

171   "I have Muslim members in my family"
      Obama interview with Al-Arabiya television, January 26, 2009.

172   "Is Arab Democracy"
      www.slate.com/id/2145892/.

173   the country's more radical religious groups
      For more on Turkey's radical Islamists, see Ely Karmon, "Radical
      Islamic Political Groups in Turkey," *Middle East Review of Interna-*
      *tional Affairs* 1, no. 4 (1997); available online at http://meria.biu.ac.il/
      journal/1997/issue4/jv1n4a2.html.

# Select Bibliography

Abbas, Tahir, ed. *Muslim Britain: Communities Under Pressure*. London: Zed, 2005.

AlSayyad, Nezar, and Manuel Castells, eds. *Muslim Europe or Euro-Islam*. Lanham, Md.: Lexington Books, 2002.

Amin, Samir, et al., eds. *Transforming the Revolution*. New York: Monthly Review Press, 1990.

Anderson, Benedict. *Imagined Communities: Reflections on the Origin and Spread of Nationalism*. London: Verso, 2006.

Asad, Talal. *On Suicide Bombing*. New York: Columbia University Press, 2007.

Barrett, David, et al., eds. *World Christian Encyclopedia: A Comparative Survey of Churches and Religions—AD 30 to 2200*. London: Oxford University Press, 2001.

Berryman, Phillip. *The Religious Roots of Rebellion*. New York: Orbis, 1984.

Buechler, Steven M. *Social Movements in Advanced Capitalism*. New York: Oxford University Press, 2000.

Burke, Edmund. *The Works of the Right Honourable Edmund Burke*. London: Oxford University Press, 1907.

Carpenter, Joel A., and W. R. Shenk. *Earthen Vessels: American Evangelicals and Foreign Missions, 1880–1980.* Grand Rapids, Mich.: Eerdmans, 1990.

Carroll, James. *Crusade: Chronicles of an Unjust War.* New York: Metropolitan Books, 2004.

Chanda, Nayan. *Bound Together: How Traders, Preachers, Adventurers, and Warriors Shaped Globalization.* New Haven, Conn.: Yale University Press, 2007.

Cherry, Conrad. *God's New Israel.* Upper Saddle River, N.J.: Prentice Hall, 1971.

Cohen, Robin, and Shirin M. Rai, eds. *Global Social Movements.* London: Athlone Press, 2000.

Della Porta, Donatella. *Social Movements, Political Violence, and the State.* Cambridge, England: Cambridge University Press, 1995.

Devji, Faisal. *Landscapes of the Jihad.* Ithaca, N.Y.: Cornell University Press, 2005.

Durkheim, Emile. *Suicide: A Study in Sociology.* Glencoe, Ill.: Free Press, 1951.

Ellens, J. Harold, ed. *The Destructive Power of Religion.* Vol. 1. Westport, Conn.: Praeger, 2004.

Foucault, Michel. *Discipline and Punish: The Birth of the Prison.* New York: Vintage, 1995.

———. *The History of Sexuality,* vol. 1. New York: Vintage, 1990.

Gerges, Fawaz. *The Far Enemy: Why Jihad Went Global.* Cambridge, England: Cambridge University Press, 2005.

Goldberg, Michelle. *Kingdom Coming.* New York: Norton, 2007.

Gorenberg, Gershom. *The Accidental Empire: Israel and the Birth of the Settlements, 1967–1977.* New York: Times Books, 2006.

———. *The End of Days: Fundamentalism and the Struggle for the Temple Mount.* New York: Simon and Schuster, 2001.

Hatina, Meir. *Islam and Salvation in Palestine.* Tel Aviv: Tel Aviv University, 2001.

Hedges, Chris. *American Fascists.* New York: Free Press, 2006.

Hobsbawm, E. J. *Primitive Rebels.* New York: Norton, 1959.

Hoffer, Eric. *True Believer.* New York: Harper & Row, 1951.

Holm, Hans-Henrik, and Georg Sørensen, eds. *Whose World Order?: Uneven Globalization and the End of the Cold War.* Boulder, Colo.: Westview Press, 1995.

ibn al-Matroudi, Abd al-Hakim. *The Hanbali School of Law and Ibn Taymiyya.* London: Routledge, 2006.

Jansen, Johannes J. G. *The Neglected Duty.* New York: Macmillan, 1986.

Juergensmeyer, Mark. *Global Rebellion: Religious Challenges to the Secular State, from Christian Militias to Al-Qaeda.* Berkeley: University of California Press, 2008.

———. *Terror in the Mind of God: The Global Rise of Religious Violence.* Berkeley: University of California Press, 2003.

Kanafani, Ghassan. *The 1936–39 Revolt in Palestine.* New York: Committee for a Democratic Palestine, 1978.

Kepel, Gilles. *The Revenge of God: The Resurgence of Islam, Christianity and Judaism in the Modern World.* University Park: Pennsylvania State University Press, 1994.

Kilcullen, David J. "Countering Global Insurgency." *Journal of Strategic Studies* 28, vol. 4 (August 2005): 597–617.

Lawrence, Bruce, ed. *Messages to the World: The Statements of Osama bin Laden.* London: Verso, 2005.

Lein, Yehezkel. *Land Grab: Israel's Settlement Policy in the West Bank.* Jerusalem: B'Tselem, 2002.

Lia, Brynjar. *Architect of Global Jihad: The Life of Al-Qaida Strategist Abu Musab al-Suri.* New York: Columbia University Press, 2008.

Lustick, Ian. *For the Land and the Lord: Jewish Fundamentalism in Israel.* New York: Council on Foreign Relations, 1988.

Mandaville, Peter. *Transnational Muslim Politics: Reimagining the Umma.* New York: Routledge, 2004.

Marcus, Amy Dockser. *Jerusalem 1913.* New York: Viking, 2007.

Marsden, George M. *Fundamentalism and American Culture.* New York: Oxford University Press, 2006.

———. *Understanding Fundamentalism and Evangelicalism.* Grand Rapids, Mich.: Eerdmans, 1991.

Melucci, Alberto. *Challenging Codes: Collective Action in the Information Age.* Cambridge, England: Cambridge University Press, 1996.

Mueller, John. *Overblown: How Politicians and the Terrorism Industry Inflate National Security Threats and Why We Believe Them.* New York: Free Press, 2006.

Olson, Mancur. *The Logic of Collective Action.* Cambridge, Mass.: Harvard University Press, 1965.

Pape, Robert. *Dying to Win.* New York: Random House, 2005.

Pauly, Robert J. *Islam in Europe: Integration or Marginalization?* Burlington, Vt.: Ashgate, 2004.

Reich, Walter, ed. *Origins of Terrorism*. Washington, D.C.: Woodrow
    Wilson Press, 1990.

Reid, T. R. *The United States of Europe*. New York: Penguin, 2004.

Robertson, Roland. *Globalization: Social Theory and Global Culture*. London:
    Sage, 1992.

Roy, Olivier. *Secularism Confronts Islam*. New York: Columbia University
    Press, 2008.

Sageman, Marc. *Leaderless Jihad*. Philadelphia: University of Pennsylvania
    Press, 2008.

Samad, Yunas, and Katsuri Sen, eds. *Islam in the European Union*. Oxford,
    England: Oxford University Press, 2007.

Schwartz, Michael. *Radical Protest and Social Structure*. New York:
    Academic Press, 1976.

Sizer, Stephen. *Christian Zionism: Road-Map to Armageddon?* Leicester,
    England: Inter-Varsity Press, 2004.

Smith, Anthony D. *National Identity*. Reno: University of Nevada Press, 1991.

———. *Nationalism: Theory, Ideology, History*. Cambridge, England: Polity, 2001.

———. *The Nation in History*. Hanover, N.H.: University Press of New
    England, 2000.

———. *Nations and Nationalism in a Global Era*. Cambridge, England:
    Polity, 1995.

Smith, Charles D. *Palestine and the Arab-Israeli Conflict*. Boston: St. Martin's
    Press, 2001.

Smith, Christian. *American Evangelicalism: Embattled and Thriving*. Chicago:
    University of Chicago Press, 1999.

———. *Disruptive Religion*. New York: Routledge, 1996.

Tarrow, Sidney. *Power in Movement*. Cambridge, England: Cambridge
    University Press, 1998.

Thatcher, Oliver J., and Edgar Holmes McNeal, eds. *A Source Book for
    Medieval History*. New York: Scribner's, 1905.

Tyerman, Christopher. *Fighting for Christendom: Holy War and the Crusades*.
    London: Oxford University Press, 2004.

Walzer, Michael. *Arguing About War*. New Haven, Conn.: Yale University
    Press, 2004.

Watt, W. Montgomery. *The Formative Period of Islamic Thought*. Oxford,
    England: Oneworld Publications, 1998.

Weber, Max. *Politics as a Vocation*. Minneapolis: Fortress Press, 1972.

Wilson, John. *Introduction to Social Movements*. New York: Basic Books, 1973.

# Index

PHOTO © HILARY JONES

REZA ASLAN is assistant professor of Creative Writing at the University of California, Riverside, and senior fellow at the Orfalae Center for Global and International Studies at the University of California, Santa Barbara. His first book, *No god but God: The Origins, Evolution, and Future of Islam*, has been translated into thirteen languages, short-listed for the Guardian First Book Award, and placed on Blackwell's list of the one hundred most important books of the last decade.

www.rezaaslan.com